composition
STUDIES

Volume 42, Number 1

Spring 2014

I0027836

SUBSCRIPTIONS

Composition Studies is published twice each year (May and November). Annual subscription rates: Individuals $25 (Domestic), $30 (International), and $15 (Students). To subsccribe online, please visit http://www.uc.edu/journals/composition-studies/subscriptions.html

BACK ISSUES

Some back issues from volume 13.1 and forward are available at $8 per issue. Photocopies of earlier issues are available for $3. To order or inquire about availability, see http://www.uc.edu/journals/composition-studies/subscriptions.html. More recent back issues are now available through Amazon.com. To find issues, use the advanced search feature and search on "Composition Studies" (title) and "Parlor Press" (publisher).

BOOK REVIEWS

Assignments are made from a file of potential book reviewers. To have your name added to the file, send a current vita to the Book Review Editor at ainoue@csufresno.edu.

JOURNAL SCOPE

The oldest independent periodical in the field, *Composition Studies* publishes original articles relevant to rhetoric and composition, including those that address teaching college writing; theorizing rhetoric and composing; administering writing programs; and, among other topics, preparing the field's future teacher-scholars. All perspectives and topics of general interest to the profession are welcome. We also publish Course Designs, which contextualize, theorize, and reflect on the content and pedagogy of a course. Contributions to Composing With are invited by the editor, though queries are welcome (send to compstudies@uc.edu). Cfps, announcements, and letters to the editor are most welcome. Composition Studies does not consider previously published manuscripts, unrevised conference papers, or unrevised dissertation chapters.

SUBMISSIONS

For submission information and guidelines, see http://www.uc.edu/journals/composition-studies/submissions/overview.html.

Direct all correspondence to:

> Laura Micciche, Editor
> Department of English
> University of Cincinnati
> PO Box 210069
> Cincinnati, OH 45221–0069
> compstudies@uc.edu

Composition Studies is grateful for the support of the University of Cincinnati.

©2013 by Laura Micciche, Editor
Production and printing is managed by Parlor Press, www.parlorpress.com.
ISSN 1534–9322.
Cover art by Giovanni Weissman and design by Gary Weissman.

http://www.uc.edu/journals/composition-studies.html

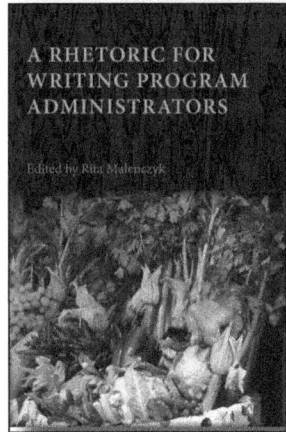

2013–2014 Reviewers

A journal is only as good as its reviewers. We acknowledge and celebrate the dedication, good will, and expertise of our generous reviewers:

Lois Agnew, Syracuse Univ.
Kara Poe Alexander, Baylor Univ.
Tom Amorose, Seattle Pacific Univ.
Janet Bean, Univ. of Akron
Nicholas Behm, Elmhurst College
Patrick Bizzaro, Indiana Univ. of Pennsylvania
Resa Crane Bizzaro, Indiana Univ. of Pennsylvania
Robert Brooke, Univ. of Nebraska–Lincoln
Christopher Burnham, New Mexico State Univ.
Paul Butler, Univ. of Houston
Jami Carlacio, Borough of Manhattan Community College
Shannon Carter, Texas A&M Univ.–Commerce
James Comas, Middle Tennessee State Univ.
Paul Cook, Indiana Univ. Kokomo
Ilene Crawford, Southern Connecticut State Univ.
Andrea Deacon, Univ. of Wisconsin–Stout
William DeGenaro, Univ. of Michigan–Dearborn
Sidney Dobrin, Univ. of Florida
Doug Downs, Montana State Univ.
Dylan Dryer, Univ. of Maine
Patricia Dunn, Stony Brook Univ.
Michelle Eble, East Carolina Univ.
Lynnell Edwards, Spalding Univ.
Dana Elder, Eastern Washington Univ.
Heidi Estrem, Boise State Univ.
Paul Feigenbaum, Florida International Univ.
Tom Friedrich, SUNY Plattsburgh
Christy Friend, Univ. of South Carolina
Erica Frisicaro–Pawlowski, Daemen College
Cathy Gabor, Univ. of San Francisco
Chris Gallagher, Northeastern Univ.
Alice Gillam, Univ. of Wisconsin–Milwaukee
Brenda Glascott, CSU–San Bernardino
Maureen Daly Goggin, Arizona State Univ.
Heather Graves, Univ. of Alberta
Mark Hall, Univ. of Central Florida
Wayne Hall, Univ. of Cincinnati
Dana Harrington, East Carolina Univ.
Joe Harris, Univ. of Delaware
Paul Heilker, Virginia Polytechnic Institute and State Univ.

Brooke Hessler, Oklahoma City Univ.
Charlotte Hogg, Texas Christian Univ.
Deborah Holdstein, Columbia College
Sue Hum, Univ. of Texas–San Antonio
Emily Isaacs, Montclair State Univ.
Rebecca Jackson, Texas State Univ.
Dale Jacobs, Windsor Univ.
Kristine Johnson, Xavier Univ.
Susan Kirtley, Portland State Univ.
Christie Launius, Univ. of Wisconsin–Oshkosh
Carrie Leverenz, Texas Christian Univ.
Cynthia Lewiecki–Wilson, Miami Univ.
Drew Loewe, St. Edward's Univ.
Min–Zhan Lu, Univ. of Louisville
Patricia Lynn, Framingham State Univ.
Richard Marback, Wayne State Univ.
Lisa McClure, Southern Illinois Univ. Carbondale
Moriah McCracken, St. Edward's Univ.
Lisa Meloncon, Univ. of Cincinnati
Geoffrey Middlebrook, Univ. of Southern California
Clyde Moneyhun, Boise State Univ.
Tracy Morse, East Carolina Univ.
Joddy Murray, Texas Christian Univ.
Jon Olson, Penn State Univ.
Peggy O'Neill, Loyola Univ.
Stacey Pigg, Univ. of Central Florida
Jeff Rice, Univ. of Kentucky
Nathaniel Rivers, Saint Louis Univ.
Duane Roen, Arizona State Univ.
Jeanne Rose, Penn State Berks
Hannah Rule, Univ. of Cincinnati
Raúl Sánchez, Univ. of Florida
Barbara Schneider, Univ. of Toledo
Carol Severino, Univ. of Iowa
Wendy Sharer, East Carolina Univ.
Steve Sherwood, Texas Christian Univ.
Shari Stenberg, Univ. of Nebraska–Lincoln
Donna Strickland, Univ. of Missouri
Kathryn Trauth Taylor, Purdue Univ.
Stephanie Vie, Univ. of Central Florida
Kathleen Welch, Univ. of Oklahoma
Vershawn Ashanti Young, Univ. of Kentucky
Janet Zepernick, Pittsburgh State Univ.

composition STUDIES

Volume 42, Number 1

Spring 2014

Book Reviews

From the Editor

"What's the best part of your job?" A student in advanced composition asked me this question last week. Without hesitation, I told her the collaborative opportunities are by far the most rewarding aspects of being an English professor. The chance to sit down and talk with students about their ideas; write with colleagues; dream up curricular innovations with collaborators; and work with authors, reviewers, copyeditors on this journal—these are the moments when I feel most excited about being *at work*.

Collaboration encompasses a lot: structured relationships, intentional partnerships, accidental convergences, imperceptible groupings. Sculpture professor and visual artist Adam Frelin gets at nearly all of these associations in his "Composing With" contribution. Describing his process of composing a video that documents a performance piece, Frelin attributes the final product to diverse collaborative partners: research, wine, coincidence, props, and luck, among them.

Collaboration emerges again in the three articles featured in this issue, though in different contexts and for varying ends. Marsha Lee Baker, Eric Dieter, and Zachary Dobbins advance a pedagogy of mutual inquiry, influenced by Wayne Booth's work, based on ethical trust and emphathic listening. Jo Mackiewicz and Isabelle Thompson present findings from their quantitative analysis of tutoring strategies, bringing into focus cognitive and motivational scaffolding approaches to tutoring. And Matthew Vetter describes a partnership between librarians, comp teachers and students, and Wikipedia ambassadors, which culminates in student-edited Wikipedia pages as well as enhanced student motivation to publish in this messy, living archive. All three articles address the ways in which teaching, tutoring, and writing are entangled practices, involving multiple partners and relations.

In fact, this idea also informs the course design by Tabetha Adkins and Connie Meyer, which details a program for Korean students enrolled in basic writing courses at Texas A&M University–Commerce. The program draws on insights from writing about writing pedagogy, theories of rhetorical dexterity, and models of sheltered instruction. Players in this collaboration include classroom and lab instructors, writing center tutors, the director of first-year writing, the department linguistic specialist, students, and university administrators. Distributed agency, indeed!

This issue hosts the inaugural installment of an occasional section called "Where We Are," which brings together a group of scholar-teachers to address a current, compelling issue in the field. Here focused on the state of digital publishing in rhetoric and composition, this installment features short pieces by editors of digital journals and a digital book series. Contributors help us take the temperature of the field in relation to digital publishing, addressing a range of issues along the way: sustaining a digital press; preparing graduate students to contribute to and sustain digital scholarship; reframing composing through the interactive relationship between rhetoric, design, and code; valuing experimental, imaginative, pedagogical, and collaborative responses to the ever-changing publishing landscape; considering digital publishing potentialities alongside object-oriented composing practices; and taking account of shifting argumentation styles, authority constructs, and accessibility issues. The writers collectively make clear that we can no longer consider (if "we" still do) digital publishing as niche or novel. We hope you will find the pieces, and the section, inspiring and relevant to our profession. Our next installment of "Where We Are," slated for Fall 42.2, will focus on disability and accessibility, with contributions from Elizabeth Brewer, Jay Dolmage, Cynthia Lewicki-Wilson, Margaret Price, Cynthia Selfe, Tara Wood, and Melanie Yergeau.

This issue also includes timely book reviews by Gretchen Dietz and Kevin Moore, and review essays by Carl Withaus and Shakil Rabbi. The books under review address a range of issues—codeswitching, digital technology and participatory culture (closely aligned with "Where We Are"), composing in diverse genres, and theorizing rhetorical history. Together these reviews present a cross-section of the diverse research agendas that span the field.

We hope to represent such diverse research in the pages of future issues. To that end, we look forward to receiving new work from you, our readers. For complete submission (and subscription) information, visit our website at http://www.uc.edu/journals/composition-studies.html. We're also on Facebook (https://www.facebook.com/CompositionStudiesJournal) and Twitter (https://twitter.com/CompStudiesJrnl). The deadline for our upcoming special issue on Comics, Multimodality, and Composition, guest edited by Professor Dale Jacobs, is August 1, 2014; see our website for details.

Finally, in the spirit of collaboration, and beginning with this spring issue, we list in the front matter our manuscript reviewers who have given their time and expertise during 2013–14 (listings will be published in spring issues henceforth). We are humbled and cheered by the good will reviewers have extended to prospective contributors. Really, this journal would not be possible without the good work of our community members: we are indebted to you! While working the exhibit hall at the 2014 CCCCs in Indianapolis, we were amazed by the number of people who stopped by to say that they appreciated reviewers' comments and found the review process to be affirming and productive. We thank all who gave generously and feelingly toward the advancement of ideas in our field.

L.M.
Cincinnati, Ohio
March 2014

Composing With

Bridging the Gap

Adam Frelin

Making artwork is more logical than most people realize. By saying this, I know that I am destroying the fantasy of the impulsive, passionate creator. Artists have their set schedules, their preferred ingredients, and their tested formulas. For many visual artists, making art is an exercise in trying to find the logic that is conceivably hidden within each new project or piece. Occasionally it is an elegant and effortless act. More often, teasing out a project's internal logic is a layered and convoluted journey full of dead ends and pitfalls. I'll tell you about one of those recent journeys.

In 2012, I completed a piece that's been showing regularly in galleries and museums, *Terranauts*: a 10-minute video piece, though I like to think that it's more of a short story, possibly a long poem (see the video and other images at http://www.adamfrelin.com/works/Terranauts-72/). The central element in the video is a cardboard box large enough for two people to sit inside and peer out through a cutout window. The box is used as a viewing chamber by a young Latino couple who drag it all over Los Angeles to frame the landscape.

Though the bulk of my artistic practice is in video, I am in fact a sculpture professor. Rather than exhibit my sculptures as art objects, I integrate them, as props, into stories such as this one.

To understand the inspiration for *Terranauts,* we have to go to Japan. About ten years ago, I received a fellowship to research garden design in Kyoto. While there I learned that many Japanese gardens are meant to be viewed through a building, which acts as a framing device. Something as simple as a rectangle cut out of a wall distills all life seen through it into a digestible, living image. It's photography and film done simpler and, in my opinion, better. For years I wanted to take advantage of this strategy but couldn't think of anything to make, short of constructing my own building. Long after my initial inspiration, I found myself in Los Angeles for the summer with nothing to work on, so I thought I would finally try to create my own cardboard version of a viewing chamber. I spent weeks testing out its scale and the best way to construct it. Once it was made, I realized that I had other problems.

> Why a cardboard box? And why this size?
> Why does it have a window cut out of one end?
> Who is going to move it around?
> And why are we in L.A.?!

If such a prop is going to play an integral role in the narrative, its logic has to be believable. My videos often contain little to no dialogue, so each piece needs to be capable of conveying meaning through image and action alone.

At this point, I started doing some research, which for me includes everything from long-winded discussions to multiple glasses of wine. I think it was the latter that helped me stumble onto the website for the Jet Propulsion Laboratory, which happens to be located in the greater Los Angeles area. My research led me to the Kepler spacecraft launched by NASA in 2009 to search for habitable planets. Slowly I began to create a bridge between that mission and my cardboard box.

If some of the parts for the satellite were hypothetically shipped to the lab in a box that had labeling on it that clearly described its contents, and if that empty cardboard box was discovered in the garbage after the parts were removed (with the front of the box having been cut out in a strategic way that happened to create a window), our young couple could use it as a means for exploring their own earthly habitat of Los Angeles. Brilliant!

Ok, not brilliant, but this logic helped me tie together several loose ends, namely the

1. need for a big cardboard box with a viewing window,
2. role of the young couple using it as a framing device,
3. similarities and differences between the couple's and the lab's aim of exploration, and
4. need to shoot the video in L.A.

Of course there are parts to this narrative that don't exactly make sense (like, why would million-dollar spacecraft parts be shipped in a cardboard box?), but it has enough of the right kind of logic to allow viewers to become immersed in the story.

But how can I tell?

It has to do with something I was told in art school never to say: *It feeeeeels right.* After all options have been considered, materials and equipment have been tested, and references have been checked, there often remains a gap in the logic of the piece. I choose to bridge this gap based on what feeeeeels like the best thing to do, and then I jump. Sometimes I make it, and sometimes I don't. But this feeling, call it intuition, is a hard-earned gift. It's the result of decades of work, making piece after piece until a voice begins to emerge, or better yet becomes submerged, internalized.

Articles

The Art of Being Persuaded: Wayne Booth's Mutual Inquiry and the Trust to Listen

Marsha Lee Baker, Eric Dieter, and Zachary Dobbins

This article examines Wayne C. Booth's legacy as a teacher and scholar through the concept of rhetoric as mutual inquiry that he develops from *Modern Dogma and the Rhetoric of Assent* (1974) through *The Rhetoric of Rhetoric* (2004). Booth's work connects the political and pedagogical in pragmatic and productive ways that serve the humanitarian ambition to teach civic literacy while alleviating potential anxieties over politicizing rhetoric and writing classrooms. This article turns on Booth's pivotal question "When should you and I change our minds?" emphasizing that learning how to *be* persuaded is as important a critical and civic capacity as learning how to persuade. After suggesting limitations with the Aristotelian appeals for persuading oneself, we discuss Booth's definition of rhetoric as "the art of discovering warrantable beliefs and improving those beliefs in shared discourse" and the ways it minimizes logos-centric arguments while emphasizing refreshed approaches to engaging ethos and pathos. Finally, we illustrate a pedagogy that helps students develop ethical trusting and empathetic listening with implications for a rhetorical education and public discourse that are mutually nonviolent and sustainable.

This article examines Wayne C. Booth's legacy as a teacher and scholar through the concept of rhetoric as mutual inquiry that he develops between 1974, in *Modern Dogma and the Rhetoric of Assent,* and *The Rhetoric of Rhetoric* in 2004.[1] As we approach the tenth anniversary of Booth's passing in 2005, his work persists as an insightful guide for connecting the political and pedagogical in pragmatic and productive ways. As we seek to demonstrate, Booth's work lives up to the deep humanitarian ambitions of many composition teachers to promote citizenship while alleviating potential anxieties over politicizing writing classrooms. To be clear, the authors are interested not in teaching any particular political outcome, but rather particular political behaviors. Instead of expecting students to choose among partisan views, we aim to teach them how to engage in transparent, constructive, and nonviolent civil discourse. We further seek teachable moments in which students experience the relevance of civil discourse to their lives and the desire to contribute to it. In short, through Booth's legacy composition teachers can help students decide when and how to change their own minds without telling them what to think.

To illustrate the power of asking students to persuade themselves in composition courses, we begin with the frequently divisive issue of sexual identity. In first-year writing courses on one of our university campuses, the merits of logos seem largely irrelevant to students raised to believe that homosexuality is something regarded as a sin, disease, or crime. For these students, reasonable or factual justifications in defense of homosexuality sound driven by emotions and mere rhetoric. The same rebuke of logos comes from students raised to believe that homosexuality is something regarded as a genetic marker and a political identity. For them, any defense of heteronormativity sounds equally driven by emotions and mere faith. Both groups often perceive disagreements as attacks on the authority figures of their upbringing who instilled these beliefs in them, further escalating their emotional defensiveness. The possibility of civil discourse between these groups, much less any potential for changing minds, is slim.

One instructional response to this predicament is to avoid the topic altogether, but such a choice eliminates the opportunity for cultivating civic literacy. Well-intentioned instructors also often respond by encouraging students to stick to what they know and leave out what they feel, inadvertently shutting down further discussion. Rather than avoiding the topic, the class simply avoids their feelings, limiting their arguments to evidence, and their evidence to incontrovertible facts. Yet, how can students stick to the so-called facts when those facts exist in part because of the authorities and emotions through which they are constituted? Is it a fact, for instance, that God condemns/condones homosexuality, or that nature abhors/accepts homosexuality, and why in the first place is one appealing to God or to nature? As the phrase goes back home, it's hard to talk folks out of something they've never been talked into. Even when instructors widen the terrain for talk, inviting debate over controversial issues, the invitation often includes a disclaimer decoded by students as a call for appealing primarily to logos: people are most often persuaded by objectivity. Not unsound advice, though discussion may crumble under such caveats, since students may stop talking (and thinking) once they realize their beliefs may be quickly dismissed as unconvincingly subjective. Certainly it can seem pointless to listen to classmates' thoughts after realizing the discussion comes down to a deadlock between your facts or mine. Will students even participate in discussions like this? Why should they?

To reinvigorate scenarios like this one, in this article we suggest redirecting students from questions like "How can I change *your* mind?", which we see as typical in rhetoric and composition classrooms, and towards a question like "What changes *my* mind?", which falls closer to Booth's view of rhetoric as mutual inquiry. Booth centralizes the question "When should you and I change our minds?" in his theory and practice for a modern rhetoric education (*Dogma* 12), emphasizing that mutual inquiry gives merit and courage to self-inquiry. It comes as no surprise, then, that Booth does not endorse a rhetoric primarily focused on changing other people's minds: "The supreme purpose of persuasion . . . could not be to talk someone else into a preconceived view; rather it must be to engage in mutual inquiry or exploration," Booth critiques, and then offers, "Whatever imposes belief without personal engagement becomes inferior to whatever makes mutual exchange more likely" (*Dogma* 137). As Booth well knew, talking someone else into a preconceived view often amounts to some form of coercion. At the very least, argumentation that privileges persuasion over mutual inquiry reinforces a competition that can silence some rhetors or leave others less heard.

Changing minds in the composition classroom can mean that students realize that they and their peers construct differing positions with similar processes of reasoning. Such a realization requires developing a metacognitive awareness of argument as it happens, of rhetor *qua* rhetor in real time, and "exploring the ways we think about the ways we think" (Booth, "Mere Rhetoric" 331). It does not, however, require students to aim for persuasion, working to get each other to abandon their own and adopt others' positions. In fact, following Booth, we argue that teaching students how to be persuaded is as essential a critical and civic capacity as teaching them how to persuade. Being persuaded requires mutual inquiry, which involves trust and empathy, capacities Booth considers crucial to civic life. Persuading others depends on distinctions, sometimes constructed in reductive win-lose or right-wrong binaries, that accentuate competition at some expense to these Boothian capacities.

Concerns about civil discourse are what prompted Booth to write *Modern Dogma*. Booth was troubled by other people's inability to listen to each other during an era of intense and sometimes violent protest, and he also was frustrated by his own inability to help University of Chicago administrators, faculty, and students move through ideological impasses with less vitriol and more understanding than any side was then demonstrating. *Modern Dogma*'s introduction recollects Booth's puzzlement about why students could not "get themselves heard," why faculty and administrators were unable "to make their responses intelligible," and what to make of the "unspoken assumptions that beclouded" virtually everything everyone was saying (ix). Working through this dilemma, Booth recalls a similar frustration in his "first losing battles with freshman composition," a course predicated on privileging fact and isolating value "so that the goal of all thought and argument [was] to emulate the purity and objectivity and rigor of science, in order to protect oneself from the errors that passion and desire and metaphor and authority and all those logical fallacies lead us into" (88). During this period of political and pedagogical conundrums Booth describes, nobody was changing anybody's mind, least of all their own.

In *Modern Dogma,* Booth defines rhetoric as "the art of discovering warrantable beliefs and improving those beliefs in shared discourse" (xiii; see also 10-11).[2] Three decades later, by the time Booth writes his manifesto for rhetoric education, *The Rhetoric of Rhetoric,* he advances what he terms "listening-rhetoric" as the "whole range of communicative arts for reducing misunderstanding *by paying full attention to opposing views*" (10, emphasis added).[3] Mutually inquiring rhetors work with a techne of listening, an "art of probing what [people] believe they ought to believe, rather than proving what is true according to abstract methods" (*Dogma* xiii). This distinction is important: it is probing for the "oughts," rather than proving a truth via sheer objectivity, that urges understanding, and Booth provides a range of rhetorical terminology throughout his corpus for the "warrantable beliefs" rhetors are "discovering" and "improving." For instance, when questioning whether the differences between science and religious faith are as irreconcilable as some suggest, he asks, "If disputants really probed for shared warrants—if they really listened—would they find far fewer real differences?" His question implies the answer: yes, they would no doubt uncover some already shared warrants, or "shared unquestionable convictions . . . assumptions, commonplaces, topoi, firm platforms, or 'places' on which they stand" ("Rhetoric, Science, Religion" 270). Booth further emphasizes place: "In the ancient terminology of rhetoricians, we seek to discover the topics, the topoi, the places or locations on which or *in* which, a shared inquiry can take place" ("Mere Rhetoric" 318, original emphasis). Discovering warrantable beliefs, then, often entails uncovering hitherto unrecognized, or at least unacknowledged, common ground among rhetors. Through shared inquiry, the rhetors involved choose which beliefs they will probe together, using listening as their dowsing rod to discover what has been involved in creating and sustaining beliefs held by one another and themselves. Warrantable beliefs improve, and misunderstanding decreases, as interlocutors move beyond the surface of what the beliefs are and into the deeper territory of figuring out why others hold those beliefs, how they articulate them, and why they articulate them as they do. Addressing those what, how, and why questions equally with oneself, we emphasize, is key to changing one's mind.

Mutual inquiry is by design a dynamic and perpetual process, one that neither intends nor requires automatic, eventual, or permanent agreement. What one is willing to warrant can, will, and should change as experience, *kairos*, and knowledge change. Our opening scenario from a college campus illustrates one of many kinds of rhetorical situations highly unlikely to yield persuasion (i.e., one student convincing another to take on a supposed winning or right view). Rather than persuasion this situation calls for mutual inquiry, through which students can metacognitively engage their own beliefs and consider whether and to what extent they should change their own minds. So we call for teaching students to observe *how,* instead of *what,* their classmates think. Of course some students will resist or struggle with trying not to focus on another person's thoughts; many are comfortably and capably accustomed to making arguments against what another person thinks. But so, too, do some students prefer to find how other people's minds work, especially among their peers, and they want to compare notes and figure out resolutions to problems together. In either case, teaching mutual inquiry equips students with stronger and more flexible cognitive abilities, an outcome most students are glad to claim at least in the long run.

As the opening scenario further suggests, a common pedagogical strategy for guiding substantively difficult conversations is to invoke logos, appropriately enough. The Aristotelian appeals of logos, ethos, and pathos are some of the most enduring concepts from classical rhetoric and are a useful heuristic for deliberative writing and reading in contemporary writing instruction and rhetorical criticism. But despite the ubiquity and clear usefulness of the appeals, we admit a discomfort with how easily they can slip into a strict taxonomy of persuasive techne, a precise schema of suasive strategies that each perform distinct categorical work. This slippage does not serve mutual inquiry well, nor does the discreteness with which classical appeals typically are introduced and defined. We share in the frustrations of M. Jimmie Killingsworth, who has recently argued for a "revised model" of appeals ("Rhetorical Appeals" 249).[4] That said, Killingsworth identifies as a "problem" in deploying the appeals something we perceive as an essential insight: "The problem is that authors demonstrate their character in every utterance; likewise, the emotions of the audience might attach to just about anything in a text; and without reasoning, nothing would make sense" (*Appeals* 25). It is precisely because ethos and pathos saturate everything in an argument that we are drawn to Booth's mutual inquiry: It acknowledges and engages a more explicitly interdependent, mutually inclusive, and mutually gratifying relationship between what is known and felt. The places of mutual inquiry are not dominated by logos, and reasoning and reasons are not confined to it. Logos provides arguments with factual and judicious evidence, of course, but this appeal is also a heuristic for exploring someone's entire range of thought, including thinking rooted in authority and emotions. Logos is part of a process people engage in persistently, if not always resolutely, producing rhetorical reasons the certitude of which are rarely absolute or empirical. Perhaps most crucial to mutual inquiry, logos is epistemologically dependent on both ethos and pathos. Not only are the three appeals taken as evidentiary proofs, they are *a priori* forms of imperative reasoning. Which is to say, Booth's warrantable beliefs are not logos-centric: they do not invest in or derive from the fact-value and rational-irrational binaries of typical Western thought that supersede all else in favor of pure reason (see *Dogma* 14-21).[5]

When students can barely listen to each other, much less imagine changing their minds, teachers witness what can happen when difficult conversations do not involve working with the appeals synchronously. What shuts down these conversations is not the presence of ethos and pathos, but a failure to bring the persuasive potential of these two appeals into full consideration. Part of our goal in this article is to illustrate how ethos and pathos are not simply complements to logical reasoning but are necessary forms of reasoning in their own right. Because, as their name suggests, warrantable beliefs should not be ruled either acceptable or unacceptable before engaging in mutual inquiry, and because engaging logos, ethos, and pathos is recognized as perpetual blending, Booth's work necessarily provides fresh approaches for teachers and students conceptualizing and engaging ethos and pathos. Therefore, we offer the following extended discussion of ethical trusting and empathetic listening—or as we title it, "the trust to listen"—as essential political behaviors for students learning to become participants in civil discourse.

What makes Booth's concept of ethos iconoclastic and functional for students and teachers is its nonnegotiable inclusion of the ethos of the audience alongside that of the rhetor in rhetorical situations. "You and I are remade as we encounter the remakings," Booth exhorts (*Rhetoric* 17-18). The high probability for being "remade" underwrites Booth's conviction that audiences and rhetors possess corresponding obligations to each other during rhetorical encounters. It is not surprising, then, that he defines his concept of ethos with the separate yet similar terms, *ethos* and *ethical*: "The word 'ethical' may mistakenly suggest a project concentrating on quite limited moral standards," whereas he is "interested in a much broader topic," namely, "the entire range of effects on the 'character' or 'person' or 'self'" (*Company* 8). For Booth, ethical criticism is obviously much more, and much more interesting, than judging the morals of rhetors and their discourse (though certainly moral judging occurs). Booth admits that ethical criticism "must cover all qualities in the character, or ethos, of authors and readers, whether these are judged as good or bad" (8). Ethical appraisals are not limited to the ethos of the rhetor, but include another "center for ethical criticism," namely the ethos of audiences, and their "responsibilities" to rhetors (9). Ethos, then, is a crosspollination between rhetors and audiences, and criticism is the act of inquiring into and judging those crosspollinations via a process of discovering, improving, and sharing.

While he recognizes the importance of an audience's critical and personal impressions, Booth nonetheless urges audiences to remain intentionally aware of when their ethos may "violate" the rhetor's, thus ignoring responsibility to the rhetor to be a coequal "center for ethical criticism." As Booth explains it, there is "a great deal of distinction between questions internal and external to a 'framework,'" that is, between how rhetors and audiences want to apprehend arguments, which gives rise to his division between understanding and overstanding texts (*Critical* 41; see also 235-56, 335-39). The goal of responsive ethical criticism is to be "committed to delaying that shift," from understanding to overstanding, "for as long as humanly possible" (41; see also 243).[6]

Booth argues for giving ourselves over to rhetors whose rhetoric is deserving of it, meeting them where they dwell; "a style that is good," he claims, "not only tends to carry us with him [or her]—it ought to," a claim he admits is "risky" (*Critical* 152). The risk, in part, is that audiences will give themselves over to rhetors who are deceitful and manipulative, who deploy bad means and ends. But the reward, in part, is a deeper recognition of the ubiquity and usefulness of the "ethical proof," which Booth defines as "the art of taking in by contagion" (*Dogma* 144). Given the unpleasant initial connotations of the word "contagion," it is constructive to remember its etymology denotes merely a touching, the pleasantness or unpleasantness of which depends on who is touching whom as rhetors and audiences come in contact with one another. A contagious ethos, that which we catch by touching one another, includes the discrete characters of both the rhetor and audience, and also the unique intellectual space created where those two distinct characters interpenetrate. In this "field of selves," Booth discovers "that there are no clear boundaries between the others who are somehow both outside and inside me and the 'me' that the others are 'in'" (*Company* 239).[7] Booth believes that "the isolated individual self simply does not, cannot exist," and warns that "[n]ot to be a *social* self is to lose one's humanity" (238, original emphasis).

This view of ethos supplies Booth's pedagogic antidote for poisonous public rhetoric (i.e., rhetoric that dissociates selves from the social field), a remedy that calls for close attention: "It is only by experiencing the sheer fun and personal profit of genuine listening, followed by really productive argument, that students can embrace the highest virtue of all: respect for others, producing trustful exchange" (*Rhetoric* 99). Here, in a single sentence, is Booth's recommendation for healthy rhetorical living and, by implication, a rhetorical education where attending to the political in the classroom connotes the exact opposite of a hyperpartisan intractability that focuses on winning at all costs, a vision of the political that citizens frequently witness in the public sphere. Instead, Booth charges teachers to work on "serving our universal need for *political* savvy" by developing our rhetorical abilities (*Vocation* 118, original emphasis). After all, Booth continues, "All our political life is conducted in one or another form of rhetoric" (118). And, in case educators miss the high stakes of this pedagogical commitment, he adds, "Working together in symbolic exchange is in fact our only alternative to tyranny" (118).[8]

Booth's own view of instructing rhetoric—that is, a rhetorical pedagogy that stresses civics, respect, and trust—is actionable, and it comes in the form of a pointed question: "How many students are learning to think about why building a community of mutual trust is better than winning this or that material reward?" (*Rhetoric* 99). For Booth it is "true that extreme public displays of commitment always say something real to anyone seriously inquiring into the values at stake in any conflict" (*Dogma* 145). Serious inquiry entails not forgetting "that the way we establish values is the way we establish anything: by earning communal validation through trying them out on other[s]" (*Dogma* 146). Based on these views, here is a guideline for turning Booth's pedagogic doctrines on trust into an ethical instructional practice: get students to (1) articulate their values, (2) test those values on others, (2.5) no, really, listen to other people's values, (3) prepare to have their own values revised as they "touch" the values of others, and, most importantly, (4) embrace the fact that changing their values will remake themselves. Each of those steps centralizes students and their texts within Booth's ethical narrative, giving them opportunities to make their arguments "not just self-satisfying," he promises, but "validate[d]" "in the courts of communal exchange" (*Dogma* 148). The fundamental classroom advice running throughout his work is to guide students toward those exchanges, while giving them the space to discover and improve for themselves the inquirable means and ends of their communities that will eventually inevitably remake them, if they are constructed respectfully, mutually, and trustfully.

A fruitful approach to teaching political savvy, then, is teaching ethos as substance, defining the character transferred into a rhetorical domain by the rhetor and audience, and also, teaching ethos as social process, defining the "contagion" between the two. Teaching ethos as a substance gives students a justification for, and guidance in, evaluating the extent to which the rhetor and audience are interpenetrated, as well as the extent to which those discrete rhetor-audience substances are made mutual and mutually made. In other words, we negotiate from individual ethical substances an agreeable social ethos, and we do so, recalling S. Michael Halloran's translation of ethos as a "habitual gathering place" (60), by dwelling in other people's ethical substances long and deep enough to understand their intentions, to understand how those intentions influence the larger public, and to understand the ways we, as the audience, are overstanding rhetors and appropriating their social effects (see *Dogma* 116 and 172). Again, it is important to note that this process of Boothian indwelling requires approaching rhetorical analysis as a metacognitive endeavor.

A collaboratively negotiated ethos sounds easier to do in theory than it is to implement in practice. But for all the attention to community and collaboration in rhetorical and pedagogical circles, pathos regularly under- and overwhelms local and global encounters. Just as rhetors do not reason together in a logos-centric vacuum, they do not reason without beliefs, convictions, or emotions: each interlocutor has his or her own backstory and unique set of values and experiences. These complex features, often (too) simply coded as pathos, shape the outcome of a rhetorical exchange as much as clashing facts or mistrust do. It is instructive, then, to examine actual instances of discomfort and dis-ease, of being close to others whom we perceive, and even prefer to perceive, as different from ourselves, and from whom we do not want to catch anything. These examinations emerge from the practical center of a composition classroom, and they illustrate the listening-empathy partnership at the core of mutual inquiry.

The ways we build on Booth's legacy in this discussion of pathos contribute to at least two of the three arguments Cheryl Glenn and Krista Ratcliffe advance in *Silence and Listening as Rhetorical Arts*: (1) by emphasizing a pedagogy of listening, we advance their claim that "the arts of silence and listening are as important to rhetoric and composition studies as the traditionally emphasized arts of reading, writing and speaking"; (2) by articulating a pedagogy for civic literacy, we demonstrate how listening "offer[s] people multiple ways to negotiate and deliberate, whether with themselves or in dyadic, small group, or large-scale situations" (2-3).[9] Furthermore, the partnership of empathy with listening involves what social psychologists call "perspective taking," an advanced cognitive capacity to understand another person's thoughts, experiences, and emotions.[10] Empathy is a civic capacity as well, as psychologist Martin Hoffman suggests when he describes empathy as "the spark of human concern for others, the glue that makes social life possible" (3). With listening as a crucial component of deliberation, empathy becomes an invaluable capacity for understanding differences, negotiating conflict, and achieving social justice. It is a partnership that requires not only imagination but also some measure of charity and, as we will explain, humility.

How do students learn how to listen to one another when values strongly clash, to empathize with people whose beliefs and actions they might preemptively rule disturbingly alien and uncontrovertibly unethical? They start by listening attentively to what others are telling them about their experiences and beliefs, as well as the roles those experiences and beliefs play in others' lives. Listening and empathy, however, can take "knowing what someone else says" to deeper dimensions by requiring the rigor of Peter Elbow's "believing game," a practice that requires "not just listening to views different from our own and holding back from arguing with them; not just trying to restate them without bias; but actually *trying* to believe them" ("Believing Game" 1-2, original emphasis). As does a contagious ethos, "the believing game asks us to scrutinize unfashionable or even repellent ideas for hidden virtues" (2).[11] In the classroom, when examining issues over which students deeply disagree, such listening encourages them to take seriously claims they might otherwise dismiss. It provides metacognitive moments when they can begin to realize that others whom they have perceived as their opposites are at the very least, like themselves, committed to their claims with reasons, convictions, and arguably the best intentions for holding them. Through listening, students can discover some of the experiences that have shaped a classmate's belief on some issue—for instance, a particular religious upbringing, a personal philosophy, or identification with a certain political ideology. With greater awareness of how these factors shape others' lives, students realize more fully how these experiences have shaped their own, which in turn might foster an awareness, if not greater respect for, epistemological, maybe ideological, pluralism.

For example, when teaching rhetorical analysis, one of us uses an intentionally abrasive argument by rock guitarist and gun rights advocate Ted Nugent: his response to the April 2007 Virginia Tech shooting, "Gun Free Zones Are Recipe for Disaster." Publishing his editorial on CNN.com just days after the shooting, in which 32 people were killed and seventeen wounded, Nugent wastes no time ridiculing his opposition with name-calling, and he makes no effort to summarize fairly his opponents' views on gun control, a range of views he sweeps aside with obvious vitriol. After listing some of the more recent shootings in gun-free zones like schools and restaurants, he asks, "Anybody see what the evil Brady Campaign and other anti-gun cults have created?" Students typically bristle at Nugent's sarcastic tone and *ad hominem* attacks; even students otherwise sympathetic to his position about gun ownership and possession find his approach counterproductive, if not mean-spirited and unfair. However, when the class is encouraged to listen to Nugent's argument as strategic and earnest, deadly serious in fact, their analyses take thought-provoking turns. The substance becomes clearer in Nugent's flashy argument for eliminating gun-free zones. Listening beyond and behind the jabs at his opposition and dismissive assessment of their views, some students begin to listen more attentively to Nugent's numerous reasons for his position: some are practical, others ethical and perhaps legal in nature, and chief among them is his belief that "armed citizens are much better equipped to stop evil than unarmed, helpless ones."

With these reasons in mind, the class then returns to Nugent's treatment of his opposition, exploring why he might feel compelled to ridicule and chastise gun control proponents. In light of his reasons, which many students still reject but now better understand, the class can now ask, "Why would he be so confrontational?" The answers are many and variously plausible: to get a rise out of his opponents, to rally his supporters, to serve his ego. One answer grows increasingly plausible the longer they consider the substance of his argument, that Nugent chastises his opposition in these ways because he considers them foolishly, gravely irresponsible, even complicit in these shootings. He believes these deaths are avoidable and that his opponents recklessly promote what he calls "feel good politics" over saving lives. Though they might disagree with Nugent, students now can understand his outrage and hostility toward the people who, in his view, promote "unarmed helplessness." Nugent's rhetoric now sounds suffused with reasons and convictions, and perhaps the best intentions, even if it is an argument that in the end they judge rhetorically unconvincing and communally damaging. By extending their initial impressions with greater efforts at listening, students are better prepared to reconsider their own thinking and rhetoric through a similar process. Further, by examining such volatile political issues (along with volatile rhetoric), students experience firsthand that the ends and means of rhetoric are many: to increase knowledge through mutual inquiry, to bear witness to their own and others' experiences, to persuade one's opposition in part by establishing common ground. They learn, too, that with every rhetorical approach, including uncivil and indecorous discourse, one develops and projects to flesh-and-blood audiences a certain character, touching their emotions and values, and eliciting from them varying degrees of trust, empathy, and respect. Nugent walks this tightrope; his audiences decide, in part, whether he drops.

To assist the larger goal of teaching productive political behaviors in rhetorical education, another benefit of teaching an argument like Nugent's is that it dramatizes rhetoric as high-stakes political practice in action. Nugent hopes to protect certain rights and to affect policy that he believes will save lives, and his rhetorical choices indicate his apparent conviction that the very project of mutual inquiry we advance in this article will not aid these results. That is, whereas the authors believe that national gun-control policy, for instance, should be developed with consideration of diverse arguments and beliefs and research, through mutual inquiry, Nugent clearly respects no policy proposed by his opposition of "spineless gun control advocates . . . squawking like chickens with their tiny-brained heads chopped off." Thus, students come to realize that if they or others wish to counter his proposals, then they should surely study his rhetoric. Otherwise, without having scrutinized his "repellent ideas" (as Elbow puts it), Nugent's critics will have missed an opportunity to discover certain "hidden virtues"—for instance, that they and Nugent share common ground when it comes to protecting lives, and that they can build on this common ground when deliberating decisions about gun policies. That Nugent is unwilling to reciprocate the trust, empathy, and respect with which students examine his beliefs, that he is concerned only with persuading his audience by whatever means, does not discount the value of the Boothian enterprise. Students have tested their beliefs alongside those that they might otherwise have avoided, and so develop a better understanding of what they believe and, consequently, of what it takes for them to defend the integrity of their own positions or to change their own minds. Furthermore, some have tested their rhetoric alongside a discourse so uncivil as to avoid it in their own.

To qualify the ways in which the trust to listen, or to state it more broadly, ethics and empathy, figures into the project of mutual inquiry, we turn to Iris Marion Young's discussion of reciprocity and moral humility. In "Asymmetrical Reciprocity," Young argues that it is both impossible to adopt positions shared by another person (i.e., reverse positions with another person), and undesirable to abandon one's own position (and identity) in an effort to identify with someone else. In part, she explains, this is because individuals are differently situated (e.g., historically, economically, and socially) and because power differentials shape (and misshape) their lived experiences as well as rhetorical situations. The uniqueness of one's position will always evade others' full understanding of that position. Therefore, Young distinguishes between "taking the perspective of other people into account, on the one hand, and imaginatively taking their positions, on the other" (341). Like Young, we believe that full intellectual inhabitancy of other people's positions, and, indeed, of their entire lives, is neither a desirable nor an attainable goal, an assertion that helps explain our advocacy of Booth's yoking of ethics and ethos in a field of selves. For Booth, as discussed above, ethical judgment extends beyond demands for automatic acquiescence of audiences to the ethos of rhetors. On the other hand, audiences should be scrupulous in their judgments to avoid conclusively labeling the moral character of rhetors (and the arguments those rhetors present) based solely on their own perceptions. Consequently, we caution against the underuse and overuse of ethos as a tool for ethical analysis because hasty ethical judgments (or a hasty lack) limit the capacity for inquiry, forcing a nonnavigable separation in discourse between interlocutors. Rather than a separation, in the middle is Booth's sweet spot, where inquiry becomes mutual because it is admitted that both audiences and rhetors are substantively present, and because time is taken to define how the substances of both audience and rhetor are made "contagious" together in an interdependent field of selves within any particular argument. Defining that field of selves goes far in understanding and explaining the motivational and kairotic origins of the argument.

We reiterate, then, that when asking students to empathize with others, we are not asking them either to invent or imagine themselves as being someone else. The approach is to take the perspective of another—to try to understand what another person believes along with why and how he or she might believe it. Young's project also cautions that the project of listening is fraught with the risk of projecting onto others our own fears, desires, and misunderstandings. To guard against and temper such projections, she advises audiences to practice "moral humility" when engaged in communicative interactions. "If I assume that there are aspects of where the other person is coming from that I do not understand," she explains, "I will be more likely to be open to listening to the specific expression of their experiences, interests, and claims. Indeed, one might say this is what listening to a person means" (350).[12] As we discuss next, teachers employ various pedagogical strategies to help students recognize their assumptions and thus potential misunderstandings.

Listening is often enacted as reading in the classroom, by having students practice summarizing, analyzing, and evaluating written discourse, a common enough approach to argumentation.[13] Listening is also standard practice in teaching research for figuring out what one's secondary sources are saying (though we might do well to refer more often and explicitly to research as the rhetorical art of listening). A multi-layered reading activity asks students to go beyond simple summary and analyze an argument before (or instead of) offering any evaluation of its effectiveness and persuasiveness. Teachers and students may benefit from acknowledging this behavior as serious play, echoing Elbow's game metaphor, especially since students often excel at evaluation but need to complement (and sometimes supplement) their personal and not always thoroughly well-informed responses with exercises in neutral summary and focused, non-evaluative analysis. By applying this task of multi-layered reading to a disparate range of discrete arguments on the same controversial issue (such as those we have extended in this article), students become more keenly aware of the many dimensions of an issue. Of course, these assignments and discussions can be complemented by the students' responses, including concessions, rebuttals, and qualifications. But to expand understanding and extend moral humility, students are encouraged to delay their responses as long as possible so as not to circumvent or shortchange the process of mutual inquiry. As Booth advises, they hold off overstanding as long as possible. Through this above process of rhetorical analysis, students accrue greater knowledge about an issue's scope and complexity. This process also helps to demonstrate Young's reminders about both the limits and merits of empathy: that all people are in fact not the same, that not all differences can be elided, and that full consensus and universal agreement may always evade humanity. Nevertheless, discrete groups of human beings can cultivate, with varying degrees of success, greater reciprocation of the trust to listen, with a goal of understanding one another more fully.

This rhetorical work also bridges gaps that some teachers and students resist crossing. They experience dis-ease with the potential difficulty of discussions and deliberations over divisive issues such as gun control. But heated and even uncivil discourse is becoming increasingly unavoidable, especially in the wake of the mass shooting at Sandy Hook Elementary School in late 2012 when national conversations about gun violence erupted, and Nugent's argument was again articulated, admonished, and even advocated in multiple venues across academic disciplines, jobs and professions, and homegrown cultures. Gun control is one among numerous matters that students qua students and students qua citizens in an American democracy likely cannot avoid thinking through without some measure of immediate, personal consequence in the short term. Furthermore, the longer-term consequences could damage rhetorical and literal livelihoods to the degree that words and weapons are deployed as means for violent ends. So, we see little benefit in teachers, as they engage students in shaping a more ethical, empathic civil discourse, shying away from difficult topics and prickly rhetors.

Projects in mutual inquiry certainly are not limited to political and media discourse, as Booth's devotion to the rhetoric of literature attests. Students also can exercise their capacities for listening and empathy through narrative fiction and other imaginative discourse, as Martha Nussbaum argues in *Cultivating Humanity*, where she urges developing a "narrative imagination," a civic capacity she describes as "the ability to think what it might be like to be in the shoes of a person different from oneself, to be an intelligent reader of that person's story" (10-11).[14] Nussbaum's narrative imagination is close to Booth's listening-rhetoric. Indeed, as Booth established in the early ground-breaking study *The Rhetoric of Fiction*, fiction is a tremendous resource for strengthening genuine abilities to listen and empathize closely. To read empathically someone's life, Nussbaum writes, is "essential to any responsible act of judgment, since we do not know what we are judging until we see the meaning of an action as the person intends it, the meaning of a speech as it expresses something of importance in the context of that person's history and social world" (11). Nussbaum further suggests that by developing narrative imaginations, people also cultivate abilities to recognize difference and to consider others' perspectives in order to explore their beliefs, interrogate their assumptions, and ultimately, understand the lives of others and themselves. Such listening extends to public deliberation and policymaking. "Understanding, for example, how a history of racial stereotyping can affect self-esteem, achievement, and love," Nussbaum reminds us, "enables us to make more informed judgments on issues relating to affirmative action and education" (88).

Consider as a case in point Russell Banks's novel *Rule of the Bone* (1995), a difficult text for many readers in part because it encourages them to sympathize with some arguably unsavory characters whose behavior (including theft, arson, and drug dealing) is at the least informed by forces substantially beyond their control (e.g., parental abandonment, sexual abuse, poverty).

Narrated by a Huck Finn-esque juvenile delinquent, this novel urges readers to imagine more fully and charitably the many factors that might contribute to drug abuse and teenage homelessness, thereby illustrating that such social problems are seldom simple and seldom simply anyone's choice. Such narratives, fictional or otherwise, seem an especially effective way of confronting students with arguments that help them engage reasoning. These arguments are not built by propositions, concessions, and rebuttals alone, but also by accruing detail and dramatizing the ways we shape values and, in turn, how values shape us. Further, such narratives effectively dramatize contested, constantly changing social values often ignored by purely rational thought; exposure to the persuasive power of these social values thereby enables students to grow more capable of recognizing themselves and other selves as complex social beings who persist, despite conflicts and differences, in no small part thanks to successes in rhetorical empathy. As Nussbaum argues, empathy is a civic capacity, one of three she promotes as the core of an ideal liberal education (9-11). Another is Socratic self-examination—the kind of rigorous reasoning about one's beliefs and values that, with trust and listening, enables one to be persuaded by raising again and again the question, "When should you and I change our minds?"

What then, by way of conclusion, are the implications of teaching writing and rhetoric through a Boothian approach? If rhetors do not, and in fact cannot, reason with logos alone, and if disagreement stems largely from conflicts of values, then it seems educators can be less anxious about politically and socially controversial issues in their classrooms, and more confident in helping students engage in deliberations that trade not only in facts but also in beliefs, feelings, and experiences. Fundamentally, educators can be more ambitious in helping students learn that the art of persuasion includes the art of *being persuaded*. Being persuaded develops capacities of self-reflection, critical examination, and empathic imagination as students engage in the trust to listen. Part of this pedagogical mission is to create learning environments that provide "whatever conditions make . . . mutual inquiry possible" (*Dogma* 137), including keeping conversation going (or reading and writing continuing) for as long as possible. Outcomes are unknown: rhetors do not know beforehand under what circumstances, for whom, and for what duration a belief will be found more or less warrantable. For Booth, as for us too, this uncertainty can yield great rhetorical riches. Rhetors engaged in mutual inquiry instantiate, Booth suggests, "a whole philosophy of how [people] succeed or fail in discovering together, in discourse, new levels of truth (or at least agreement) that neither side suspected before" (*Dogma* 11). In short, our argumentative ambitions expand as our definition of reasoning expands.

The trust to listen is heady stuff, for sure, but its practical consequences are made plain when we face the concern Booth centers, literally and philosophically, in his final book:

> Moving now to the sorry consequences of poor education in rhetoric, we arrive at a rough center for this whole book: "How neglect of rhetoric education, Rhet-Ed, threatens our lives." Any nation is in trouble if its citizens are not trained for critical response to the flood of misinformation poured over them daily. A citizenry not habituated to thoughtful argument about public affairs, but rather trained to "believe everything supporting my side" and "disbelieve everything supporting the bad side," is no longer a citizenry but a house of gullibles. (*Rhetoric* 89)

During and since the decade when Booth wrote this passage, partisan rancor, discursive indecorum, misleading media coverage, and a generally self-serving atmosphere of incivility continue to generate frequent and intense examples of this threat of neglecting rhetorical education. Students are preparing to contribute to a public discourse and civic life that can count on neither certainty nor consensus. Sometimes the best that students and teachers can hope for, Booth spent his career reminding us, is to produce understanding, reduce misunderstanding, and resist hostility. Completely avoiding dismissiveness and distrust in others, and ourselves, may be impossible and perhaps not always desirable. Nevertheless, we can habituate ourselves to default to a willingness to listen, respecting "the capacity to believe as itself an intellectual virtue" (*Dogma* 101). This back-and-forth of talking and listening and writing and reading, what Mikhail Bakhtin theorized as dialogizing in ways that resonated with Booth, is often referred to in composition classrooms as class discussion. Booth recognized the necessity of this pedagogic strategy and respected the teachers who bring it to life in rhetorical education: "rhetoric as inquiry, rhetoric as the dialogical path to mutual understanding, rhetoric as the training of active, growing rather than passive, meandering minds," he writes, "is learned in discussion, in the give-and-take that only a skilled discussion leader can elicit from a fairly small class" (Afterword 289).

Booth's emphasis on mutual inquiry in rhetorical life is exceptional not because it demands the insurmountable task of full consensus via persuasion, but because it assumes that full consensus is a rare if not impossible standard that is both unappealing and unhelpful to modern civic life. Booth's work recognizes and accounts for the violence intrinsic to a persuasion so strong it extirpates the need for persuasion because it essentially denies the possibility of an unpersuadable person. His alternative, a shared discourse through mutual inquiry, respects the power of well-crafted persuasion, reduces the pressure to constantly persuade (i.e., winning), mitigates the potential stigma of being persuaded (i.e., losing), and decreases the risk of perceiving oneself as either battering or being battered. For Booth, understanding is "the intellectual equivalent of love" (Afterword 290). Booth ultimately advocates for rhetorical education as a remedy for uncivil, counterproductive public discourse because it can pedagogically advance "rhetoric as our primary alternative to violence" (*Rhetoric* xi).[15] In other words, we need to teach rhetoric as nonviolent action.

What the authors find radical about Booth's view of rhetoric, and why his concept of mutual inquiry remains crucial to any pedagogy of civic literacy inspired (but undeterred) by the often sorry state of public discourse, is that through this art of discovering and improving warrantable beliefs Booth hopes to diffuse the bellicosity and belligerence corrosive to healthy discourse and informed deliberation. He hopes to diffuse also the cynicism that often simultaneously catalyzes and results from this conversational corrosiveness, a cynicism marked by doubt: on the one hand, the doubt that another person (i.e., my opponent) has anything warrantable to believe and, on the other, the doubt that there is any use in listening to a person if I am already quite convinced there is nothing to gain by doing so. By embracing mutual inquiry, we gain at the very least a better understanding of what we warrant as belief-worthy; we gain also the humility that helps us to guard against such cynicism and doubt; very possibly, and more profoundly, we gain also the mutual respect and trust necessary to guard against misunderstanding, coercion, and violence.

When rhetors mutually endeavor to discover and improve warrantable beliefs pertinent to particular deliberations, they have to trust that when they speak, others will listen, and vice versa. Booth, believing in this inquisitive rhetorical capacity in people, promotes what he calls a "*faith* in ethos," a defense of transparent rhetorical interactions that encourage "the importance of *trust*" which, he contends, is "too often ignored" (*Rhetoric* 64, original emphasis). Booth's emphasis on trust grows from his doggedness in treating education as a democratic-minded enterprise, and there is little surprise that, for Booth and for the authors, interlocutors ignore rhetorical trust at our own peril. From the perspective of a democratic-minded pedagogy, it is only in a state of authentic and mutual confidence that engaged rhetors and audiences achieve the most productive and least harmful level of dialogic understanding. For rhetoric and composition teachers attempting to teach students mutual inquiry, especially as a form of civic literacy, Booth's work is friendly and pragmatic, even as it sets for scholars, teachers, and citizens an exacting task of listening not just to what we each are saying, but to who we each are, and who, together, we are becoming.

Notes

1. The authors wish to thank Patricia Roberts-Miller for introducing us to each other and encouraging this project.

2. Booth's warrantable beliefs are not literally the same as Stephen Toulmin's "warrants" despite the use of a similar term. However, Booth does borrow from Toulmin's lexicon occasionally: "For simplicity, I'll follow Stephen Toulmin and call them the 'warrants' taken for granted on all sides'" ("Rhetoric, Science, Religion" 270). Additionally, Booth defines warrants as "tacit shared assumptions about standards and methods" (*Rhetoric of Rhetoric* 18).

3. Booth's final book was published contemporaneously with other works on rhetoric education for which our argument is relevant, including Sharon Crowley's *Toward a Civil Discourse: Rhetoric and Fundamentalism*; Cheryl Glenn, Margaret M. Lyday, and Wendy B. Sharer's *Rhetorical Education in America*; Paula Mathieu's *Tactics of Hope: The Public Turn in English Composition*; Roberts-Miller's *Deliberate Conflict: Argument, Political Theory, and Composition Classes*; and Nancy Welch's *Living Room: Teaching Public Writing in a Privatized World*.

4. Two of Killingsworth's major concerns with classical appeals are that "the Aristotelian terms fail to cover the variety of uses and the full suggestiveness of the concept and that the exclusive use of Aristotle's scheme often reduces the possibilities for understanding and interpreting the rhetorical strategies that could fall under the rubric of 'appeal'" ("Rhetorical Appeals" 249). He extends this critique and develops his own schema of appeals in *Appeals in Modern Rhetoric: An Ordinary-Language Approach*.

5. For a "reinforcement of decades of attacks on the fact-value distinction," Booth recommends Hilary Putnam's *The Collapse of the Fact/Value Dichotomy, and Other Essays* (*Rhetoric* 173n3).

6. For Booth, understanding and overstanding are necessary habits of critical listening if someone wants genuinely to comprehend a text. As Booth explains it, "Texts and modes for dealing with them will die unless each generation of readers can learn both the arts of recovering what texts demand and the arts of seeing through, judging, repudiating, transforming, and re-creating texts" (*Critical* 256). The order in which overstanding and understanding are employed, then, is crucial: first, understanding, which involves asking the most appropriate questions for discovering the text's (or rhetor's) intentions, followed by overstanding, which involves asking "inappropriate" questions so that audiences can appropriate those intentions for their own use. Booth discussed the pedagogic implications of teaching students these habits in an interview a few years before his death: as students "read the works," he explained, "they're involved in ethical differences and have to make judgments. If they don't, if they finally simply succumb to the sympathies demanded by the work, then they may very well end up having adopted the ethical values they shouldn't. On the other hand, if they don't succumb in some sense, they don't even 'get' the work" (Kraftchick).

7. Booth's collapsing of the rhetorical creator and the rhetorical receiver brings to mind Kenneth Burke's twin notions of consubstantiation and identification, and Burke's proclamation that "[t]he so-called 'I' is merely a unique combination of par-

tially conflicting 'corporate we's'" (*Attitudes* 264). For Burke, identification "is hardly other than a name for the function of sociality" (266).

8. Booth is an exemplar of practicing what he preaches. One of his former students, Meri-Jane Rochelson, recalls that "Wayne Booth taught by example," which she claims "was more than appropriate in a man who dedicated much of his life's work to exploring the ethos of the narrator and the ethics of narration" (37). "[F]or what is teaching," she asks, "but telling stories of one kind or another and enforcing their significance by telling them with both conviction and integrity?" (37). Rochelson adds that Booth's "pedagogy [was] unlikely to be taught through rules or guidelines" (37).

9. Glenn and Ratcliffe's *Silence and Listening as Rhetorical Arts* adds yet another contribution to the individual and collaborative legacies of these two scholars. Four of the six chapters in this collection's third part, "Praxes," directly contribute to a pedagogy of listening (see Duffey; Hinshaw; Jordan; and Stenberg). In particular, Wendy Wolters Hinshaw illustrates Ratcliffe's "'listening pedagogically'" as an act that "implicates the teacher as well as the students and reminds us to anticipate and empathize with the difficulty that anyone experiences—ourselves included—when asked to realize and potentially change our current identifications" (274). Hinshaw also involves emotions within these mutual acts (275), as do we by revitalizing pathos as a relationship between empathy and listening. Andrea A. Lunsford and Adam Rosenblatt point out similarities between Ratcliffe's "rhetorical listening" and Booth's "Listening-Rhetoric" (145-46). See also Ratcliffe's "Rhetorical Listening: A Trope for Interpretive Invention and a 'Code of Cross-Cultural Conduct.'"

10. Social psychologist Mark Davis, for example, distinguishes among different forms and degrees of empathic arousal and response, establishing a spectrum of "processes which generate empathic outcomes in the observer" at the ends of which he contrasts noncognitive processes (e.g., motor mimicry) with advanced cognitive processes, the latter including language-mediated association and role taking, or perspective taking (15-17). Referring to fellow social psychologist Martin Hoffman's own taxonomy, Davis defines role taking, or "the most advanced process," as "the attempts by one individual to understand another by imagining the other's perspective. It is typically an effortful process, involving both the suppression of one's own egocentric perspective on events and the active entertaining of someone else's" (17).

11. In a follow-up to Booth and Elbow's lively dialogue at the 2002 CCCC about the rhetoric of assent and the believing game, *College English* published their essays as a symposium (see Booth "Blind Skepticism" and Elbow "Bringing the Rhetoric of Assent").

12. This practice affirms the habit of mind that John Stuart Mill describes in *On Liberty*, where he promotes free discourse as a way to test belief and to guard against both dogmatism and the idea of anyone's infallibility (see especially Chapter 2, "Of the Liberty of Thought and Discussion").

13. Using the writing process to practice listening-rhetoric is effectively modeled in Gerald Graff and Kathy Birkenstein's *They Say/I Say* and Sharon Crowley and Michael Stancliff's *Critical Situations: A Rhetoric for Writing in Communities*, both

of which encourage students to develop their abilities to listen to other stakeholders' positions before launching their own responses.

14. Nussbaum is not alone in promoting the narrative imagination as a socially necessary mode of reasoned ethical inquiry. She is joined by, among others, pragmatist philosopher Richard Rorty and political theorist Iris Marion Young, both of whom independently argue that narratives, novels in particular, are an especially effective means of humanizing us to one another, for acknowledging and productively negotiating various conflicts and differences. See Young's "Communication and the Other: Beyond Deliberative Democracy" and Rorty's *Contingency, Irony, and Solidarity*, especially pages xvi and 94.

15. Booth was fond of referring to I.A. Richards' definition of rhetoric as "a study of misunderstanding and its remedies" (Richards 3; see Booth, *Rhetoric of Rhetoric* 41). Shaped by a century of world wars, both of these teacher-scholars embraced nonviolence as characteristic of an education in rhetoric that prepares students to contribute to a more sustainable public discourse and civil society.

Works Cited

Aristotle. *On Rhetoric: A Theory of Civic Discourse*. 2nd ed. Trans. George A. Kennedy. New York: Oxford UP, 2007. Print.

Banks, Russell. *Rule of the Bone*. New York: Harper, 1995. Print.

Booth, Wayne C. Afterword. *Rhetoric and Pluralism: Legacies of Wayne Booth*. Ed. Frederick J. Antczak. Columbus: Ohio State UP, 1995. 279-308. Print.

—. "Blind Skepticism versus a Rhetoric of Assent." *College English* 67.4 (2005): 378-88. Print.

—. *The Company We Keep: An Ethics of Fiction*. Berkeley: U of California P, 1988. Print.

—. *Critical Understanding: The Power and Limits of Pluralism*. Chicago: U of Chicago P, 1979. Print.

—. "Mere Rhetoric, Rhetorology, and the Search for a Common Learning." Jost 315-34.

—. *Modern Dogma and the Rhetoric of Assent*. Chicago: U of Chicago P, 1974. Print.

—. *The Rhetoric of Rhetoric: The Quest for Effective Communication*. Malden, MA: Blackwell, 2004. Print.

—. "Rhetoric, Science, Religion." Jost 265-78.

—. *The Vocation of a Teacher: Rhetorical Occasions 1967-1988*. Chicago: U of Chicago P, 1988. Print.

Burke, Kenneth. *Attitudes toward History*. Berkeley: U of California P, 1984. Print.

Crowley, Sharon. *Toward a Civil Discourse: Rhetoric and Fundamentalism*. Pittsburgh: U of Pittsburgh P, 2006. Print.

Crowley, Sharon, and Michael Stancliff. *Critical Situations: A Rhetoric for Writing in Communities*. New York: Pearson Longman, 2008. Print.

Davis, Mark H. *Empathy: A Social Psychological Perspective*. Boulder, CO: Westview, 1996. Print.

Duffey, Suellynn. "Student Silences in the Deep South: Hearing Unfamiliar Dialects." Glenn and Ratcliffe 293-303.

Elbow, Peter. "The Believing Game or Methodological Believing." *Journal for the Assembly for Expanded Perspectives on Learning* 14 (2009): 1-11. Web. 20 Jan. 2013.

—. "Bringing the Rhetoric of Assent and the Believing Game Together—and Into the Classroom." *College English* 67.4 (2005): 388-99. Print.

Glenn, Cheryl, and Krista Ratcliffe, eds. *Silence and Listening as Rhetorical Arts*. Carbondale: SIUP, 2011. Print.

Glenn, Cheryl, Margaret M. Lyday, and Wendy B. Sharer, eds. *Rhetorical Education in America*. Tuscaloosa: U of Alabama P, 2004. Print.

Graff, Gerald, and Cathy Birkenstein. *They Say/I Say: The Moves That Matter in Academic Writing*. New York: Norton, 2006. Print.

Halloran, S. Michael. "Aristotle's Conception of Ethos, or If Not His Somebody Else's." *Rhetoric Review* 1.1 (1982): 58-63. Print.

Hinshaw, Wendy Wolters. "Making Ourselves Vulnerable: A Feminist Pedagogy of Listening." Glenn and Ratcliffe 264-77.

Hoffman, Martin L. *Empathy and Moral Development: Implications for Caring and Justice*. Cambridge: Cambridge UP, 2000. Print.

Jordan, Jay. "Revaluing Silence and Listening with Second-Language English Users." Glenn and Ratcliffe 278-92.

Jost, Walter, ed. *The Essential Wayne Booth*. Chicago: U of Chicago P, 2006. Print.

Killingsworth, M. Jimmie. *Appeals in Modern Rhetoric: An Ordinary-Language Approach*. Carbondale: SIUP, 2005. Print.

—. "Rhetorical Appeals: A Revision." *Rhetoric Review* 24.3 (2005): 249-63. Print.

Kraftchick, Steve, and Michael Terrazas. "Wayne Booth Hits His Targets." *Emory Report* 18 September 2000. *Emory.edu*. Web. 6 Aug. 2013.

Lunsford, Andrea A., and Adam Rosenblatt. "'Down a Road and into an Awful Silence': Graphic Listening in Joe Sacco's Comics Journalism." Glenn and Ratcliffe 130-46.

Mathieu, Paula. *Tactics of Hope: The Public Turn in English*. Portsmouth, NH: Boynton/Cook, 2005. Print.

Mill, John Stuart. *On Liberty*. Ed. David Spitz. 1869. New York: Norton, 1975. Print.

Nugent, Ted. "Gun-Free Zones Are Recipe for Disaster." *CNN.com*. Cable News Network, 20 Apr. 2007. Web. 5 Aug. 2009.

Nussbaum, Martha. *Cultivating Humanity: A Classical Defense of Reform in Liberal Education*. Cambridge: Harvard UP, 1997. Print.

Putnam, Hilary. *The Collapse of the Fact/Value Dichotomy, and Other Essays*. Cambridge: Harvard UP, 2002. Print.

Ratcliffe, Krista. "Rhetorical Listening: A Trope for Interpretive Invention and a 'Code of Cross-Cultural Conduct.'" *CCC* 51.2 (1999): 195-224. Print.

Richards, I.A. *The Philosophy of Rhetoric*. New York: Oxford UP, 1965. Print.

Roberts-Miller, Patricia. *Deliberate Conflict: Argument, Political Theory, and Composition Classes*. Carbondale: SIUP, 2004. Print.

Rochelson, Meri-Jane. "Revisiting the 'Visitable Past': Reflections on Wayne Booth's Teaching After Twenty-Nine Years." *Pedagogy: Critical Approaches to Teaching Literature, Language, Composition, and Culture* 7.1 (2007): 37-48. Print.

Rorty, Richard. *Contingency, Irony, and Solidarity*. Cambridge: Cambridge UP, 1989. Print.

Stenberg, Shari. "Cultivating Listening: Teaching from a Restored Logos." Glenn and Ratcliffe 250-63.

Welch, Nancy. *Living Room: Teaching Public Writing in a Privatized World*. Portsmouth, NH: Boynton/Cook, 2008. Print.

Young, Iris Marion. "Asymmetrical Reciprocity: On Moral Respect, Wonder, and Enlarged Thought." *Constellations: An International Journal of Critical and Democratic Theory* 3.3 (1997): 340-63. Print.

—. "Communication and the Other: Beyond Deliberative Democracy." *Democracy and Difference: Contesting the Boundaries of the Political*. Ed. Seyla Benhabib. Princeton: Princeton UP, 1996: 120-35. Print.

Archive 2.0: What Composition Students and Academic Libraries Can Gain from Digital-Collaborative Pedagogies

Matthew A. Vetter

Research across disciplines in recent years has demonstrated a number of gains associated with community engagement and service-learning pedagogies. More recently, these pedagogies are filtering into digital contexts as instructors become aware of the opportunities for learning made available by online writing venues. This case study describes an assignment model that engages composition students in two specific communities: the Ohio University libraries' special collections (archives) and the online encyclopedia Wikipedia. Student-participants in this study performed original research within special collections on regional topics in order to edit and create corresponding Wikipedia articles. The study ultimately finds that this assignment can lead to an increase in students' rhetorical knowledge and motivation levels while also promoting public awareness of library resources and contributing to public knowledge via Wikipedia.

In the past few decades, innovation and research in pedagogy across academic disciplines has sought to engage students with materials and forums outside the classroom. In the field of composition, service or "community" learning—the application of student assignments to goal-oriented, community-based projects—has become an increasingly popular and pervasive manifestation of these movements. Pedagogies that value civic or community engagement (Herzberg; Weisser) are also intrinsically linked to this trend. A rhetorical education centered on public discourse can be traced back to the sophists (Jarratt), but a more recent motivation for this move away from the classroom can be found in the emergence of social-epistemic theories of language in the late 1980s and early 1990s and their application to writing and literacy studies (Bizzell; Gee; Harris). Proponents of service learning in composition offer a number of rationales for the shift towards public discourse. Community-engaged service learning furthers the pedagogical agenda of the social turn by expanding the audience for student writing and enabling the study of discourse within specific communities. Such models also allow for the crossing of cultural and class boundaries as students go beyond the immediate and often homogeneous cultures of the university (Deans). Researchers in composition studies have found that service-learning leads to increased levels of motivation, as it promotes a greater sense of responsibility on the part of students who undertake writing assignments that engage with outside audiences (Adler-Kassner, Crooks, and Watters; Feldman). The recognition and general acceptance of these educational gains has prompted scholars to begin thinking about the position of service-learning in the academy and how it might be further promoted, positioned, and sustained (Adler-Kassner, Crooks, and Watters).

Even more recently, scholars have appropriated figures as diverse as John Dewey and Jürgen Habermas as proponents for a public pedagogy (Barton; Richards). The use of these figures emerges within a slightly different context, however: digital pedagogies and the affordances of Web 2.0 technologies that allow users to interact and to produce discourse in virtual, online forums. Daniel Richards, for instance, utilizes Dewey's ethical pragmatism to argue for the capabilities of blogs as tools for civic activism. Matthew Barton, in an examination of Habermas' conception of a critical public sphere essential for participatory democracy, encourages the use of blogs, wikis, and discussion boards in the composition classroom. In the context of service and community-engagement learning, my use of "public pedagogy" is intended to evoke an educational model that moves beyond (private) educational spheres and involves students in projects that interact with one or more extra-academic publics, often for the purpose of providing opportunities for civic engagement and cultural participation.[1]

Ultimately, a move toward public pedagogies, digital or otherwise, is representative of a crucial shift of the boundaries of educational spaces, not only in composition but also across disciplines. Academic librarians and archivists, the professionals we so often work with to integrate research into student writing processes, have not been immune to this shift either. These professionals are increasingly challenging the static roles of "information-keepers" in order to find new and effective methods of engaging with their academic communities (Ismail et al.).

It is within these disparate yet connected contexts—service learning, civic engagement, digital pedagogies, and library research—that this article, which details a cross-disciplinary relationship between a writing program and a university library's archives (special collections), is situated. In the following, I describe an assignment model for cross-disciplinary, digital pedagogy I recently piloted in a junior-level composition course. This model is illustrated through a case study of a single student's experience with the project and also a class study, which examines the affordances of such a model. While the case study exemplifies the specific assignment model under examination in order to illustrate a student's negotiation of the project, the results of the larger study, including survey data and process logs, provide some insight into students' overall perceptions of the assignment. I ultimately argue that this type of learning is a productive means to increase students' rhetorical knowledge by exposing them to multiple authorities and audiences and that this, in turn, allows them to realize their own (personal) authority which is so often "denied in [traditional] school contexts" (Penrose and Geisler 515). Much of this increase in rhetorical knowledge stems from the finding that students are more motivated by community-engaged projects, a finding that extends the work of Deans and Adler-Kassner, Crooks, and Watters. This study also answers calls from these authors to begin thinking about how service learning might be positioned in the academy by examining the opportunities made available by cross-disciplinary relationships.

Finally, the model described here demonstrates the pedagogical benefits of a project that encourages *digital*, as well as physical, community engagement. Students working within this pedagogical model complete a public writing task that requires the translation and transmission of local knowledge sets to an openly accessible (online) public database, providing them with valuable insights into how knowledge is produced and shared in digital forums, as well as how to become familiar with specific digital community conventions in order to accomplish this work.

A Collaborative Effort in Curriculum Development

In early fall of 2011, I was contacted by the Head of Art and Archives for Libraries at Ohio University, a midsize public university enrolling around 20,000 undergraduate students. She was interested in the possibility of collaboratively developing a writing assignment for a course I was teaching in the upcoming term that would engage students in research in the library's archives and special collections. Students completing this assignment would be made aware of the available materials in these collections and would be able to return to them for future research endeavors.

Over the next few weeks, we developed an assignment that would accomplish this research goal and also raise awareness of special collections resources through a more public venue: the online encyclopedia Wikipedia. The encyclopedia had recently piloted its Global Education Program, a public policy initiative sponsored by the Wikimedia Foundation, which seeks to "engage students and professors across disciplines, universities and countries in using Wikipedia as a teaching tool" with the goal of "improv[ing] Wikipedia's coverage of course topics" ("Wikipedia: Education Program"). The program provides sample course designs and assignment ideas, as well as support for students in the form of "help" chat channels and online ambassadors who are available to answer questions and solve issues.

With this ultimate venue for publication in mind, we constructed a project consisting of the following processes and goals. Students would perform original research in the university archives and special collections to discover materials regarding a university-related topic and then edit a corresponding article on Wikipedia. In the process, students would develop relationships with the special collections curator whose collection they were researching, as well as with an assigned online ambassador, an experienced Wikipedian who volunteered time to assist students on the project. Ultimately, student-edited articles would help publicize and raise awareness of special collections because readers of these articles would be exposed to reference-links to the university archive's website.

The project was not designed entirely as a service to special collections and archives, however. From my perspective as a writing instructor, I was interested in using the encyclopedia as a way of teaching discourse community conventions as well as exposing students to a dynamic, social-process oriented model of knowledge construction. Because Wikipedia is built on a wiki platform, it allows multiple users to contribute to a single document while saving a record of individual contributions. Such a platform showcases collaborative writing processes, and having students observe and engage in these processes can be helpful on a number of cognitive and meta-cognitive levels, especially in terms of procedural, research and genre knowledge (Hood; Purdy; Vetter). Perhaps my most significant motivation was my desire to engage students with audiences and authorities outside the classroom, to get them to write for purposes beyond the course and teacher.

The collaborative nature of this project was influenced significantly by Kenneth Bruffee's 1984 landmark article "Collaborative Learning and the 'Conversation of Mankind'." In what is now a well-known argument for collaborative learning, Bruffee insists that we thoughtfully organize collaborative learning situations that contribute to "a genuine part of students' educational developments" (652). Bruffee is careful, however, to recognize the problematic aspects of peer group learning when he poses the following questions: "How can student peers, who are not themselves members of the knowledge communities they hope to enter, help other students to enter those communities? Isn't collaborative learning the blind leading the blind?" (646). Bruffee addresses this difficulty, partially, by emphasizing the ways that such an assumption reifies a Cartesian model of knowledge in which these peer groups are themselves unqualified to access an outside source of knowledge. If we move beyond these reductive assumptions toward a model in which we begin to value the knowledge sets students bring as well as the collaborative work they engage in to negotiate and build knowledge, we can begin to value their contributions more thoroughly.

In the collaborative, cross-disciplinary model presented in this study, my intent is both to support Bruffee's evaluation of peer-group learning as well as to insist that students benefit from the inclusion of collaborators outside their immediate peer group: special collections' curators and Wikipedia ambassadors, collaborators whose expertise and knowledge contribute to and motivate students in this project. These collaborators would also mitigate what Bruffee recognizes as the "pitfalls" of peer group learning: the "conformity, anti-intellectualism, intimidation, and leveling down of quality" that so often emerges when students depend on their peers for collaborative projects (652).

Designing the Study

In designing a pilot study that would explore the possibilities of this kind of collaborative-digital pedagogy, I was interested in the following research questions:

1. What can academic archivists and composition classes (both students and instructors) gain through collaborative, cross-disciplinary curriculum development?
2. How might students' perceptions of audience and authority differ in an assignment that attempts to accomplish public goals, one that incorporates a number of different audiences and collaborators?
3. Do students identify cross-disciplinary projects like this as more or less motivating than previous English assignments?
4. How do students respond to this type of cross-disciplinary pedagogy?

Student participants in this IRB approved study were enrolled in a junior-level, general education course—*Writing & Rhetoric II*—I taught during the winter quarter of 2012. Sixteen students overall, between the ages of 18 and 24, participated in the study. Because the study was situated within the practices and exigencies of the course, procedures for data collection followed closely the processes of the assignment. Students invented and researched topics in the library's archives and special collections after attending a presentation by curators on materials and policies of the collections. Their topic selections were limited, somewhat, to the availability of specific materials in the collections. Students then studied a corresponding Wikipedia article to find "gaps"—places they could identify as needing updating or revising. Next, students wrote a proposal letter to their assigned curator in which they described their plans for the article edit (see Appendix A for a description of the assignment sequence). These letters were followed by face-to-face interviews with the curator. Students then performed additional research and submitted a draft to their assigned online ambassador, who returned feedback concerning Wikipedia conventions. In the final segment of the assignment, students published their drafts.

Throughout the various assignment processes, I collected three sets of data. At two intervals in the assignment sequence, students wrote process logs to describe the influence of curators and ambassadors on their writing and research processes. Prompts for these process logs (see Appendix A), intentionally open-ended to avoid overly scripted responses from students, were designed to gain data about students' valuations of incorporating outside authorities in their writing processes. Additionally, after they had submitted their drafts for publication, students completed a questionnaire meant to gauge their perceptions of authority and audience, as well as their overall response to the project (see Appendix B). Students were given twenty-five minutes to answer nine open-ended, short response questions during which the instructor (myself) left the room. As stipulated by IRB, students were given the option of refusing to participate and were informed that their responses would be collected anonymously and would in no way affect their grade or standing in the course.

As all of the questions were qualitative, open-ended short responses, interpretation of the data was based on a type of thematic analysis drawn from Richard Boyatzis' *Transforming Qualitative Information*. A theme, according to Boyatzis, allows for qualitative analysis of a data set through recognition of "pattern[s] found in the information…that describe and organize possible observations [and/or] interpret aspects of the phenomenon" (vii). My use of this analytical method entailed the creation of codes or themes that commonly emerged in responses; when multiple themes emerged, all were included. For example, if a student lists two different themes in one question, such as identifying both the instructor and the Wikipedia public as significant authorities in the project, both were reported toward result totals. The qualitative data collected in this study informs the following two sections, in which I present a case study of a single student's experience navigating the project, followed by results of the larger class study, which focuses on student perceptions of authority and audience.

From Archive to Screen: Tracing One Student's Experience with the Archive Project

The project to perform archival research and improve a Wikipedia article on a university-related topic comes alive through a case study of a particular student, whom we'll call Mark. A baseball fan and journalism major, Mark became intrigued by university alumnus and professional baseball player George "Krum" Kahler, a particular interest of one of the archive curators. After hearing the curator talk specifically about the availability of materials in special collections related to this figure, Mark checked out the Wikipedia article for Kahler and discovered that it could use some work. In particular, Mark noticed a number of what he had come to think of, through class discussions and the project assignment, as gaps—omissions that might be filled in order to expand and improve the article. He noted many of these in a letter to the curator (see Appendix A for assignment prompt), excerpted below, which served the purpose of an introduction and project proposal:

> As you have seen from his Wikipedia page, the information on Kahler does not do him justice. Although his career was short and relatively average, he deserves more than merely three sentences for his biography. The information on there covers some of his general statistics such as earned run average, win-lose record, strikeout totals and birth and death dates. Needless to say, there is an enormous amount of information that could be added to this [Wikipedia article]. New sections could include his minor league career, information about his family, information on his football and basketball careers and his life after baseball.

Mark's proposal letter goes on to describe some of the materials he had already found in the library archives, including the Kahler Scrapbook, which according to Mark "gives an immense amount of information on Kahler by including articles, box scores and pictures of the athlete from his . . . high school days to his stint in the pros." Mark ends the letter by thanking the curator for his help and by expressing excitement about the project's goals. "Since Kahler was seen as a local hero," writes Mark, "it also adds more motivation to tell his story to the general audience." Such an attitude can tell us a lot about how students become motivated in research situations where there is a genuine audience as well as subjects they are invested in. Mark's investment in the research topic, and the relationship he formed with the curator who was also heavily invested, led to his motivation to share that interest with a larger audience. Later in the project, in one of his process logs, Mark wrote the following about the motivation he felt working with the curator one-on-one: "[The curator] sat down and showed me the information available at the Mahn Center along with giving me additional sources of his own [to] use. The excitement and enthusiasm he has for my subject has been rubbing off on me as well."

But Mark's comments are also evocative on another level. Because the project involved working across disciplines to collaborate with curators of special collections, students were able to access research materials that are not, by definition, broadly accessible to a larger audience. Working with these materials and making them more public allows students to participate first-hand in a process of research that goes beyond synthesis and argument. Mark, as well as his classmates, was able to share information with a public audience that was previously only accessible to visitors of the archive. In doing so, these students were also able to witness how digital technologies are changing the way information is created, stored, and made public, to re-imagine what an archive can look like in the twenty-first century.

Yet Mark's process on this project did not stop at his interactions with the special collections curator. As part of the collaborative nature of this assignment, Mark also interacted and worked with a Wikipedia "ambassador," an experienced Wikipedian who volunteered time to help students learn, employ article conventions, and participate in the encyclopedia's development. Working with an ambassador allowed students to come to terms with specific writing conventions of Wikipedia and to translate their archival research into a format acceptable to the Wikipedia community. In particular, Mark recognizes the significance of the ambassador's support in relation to learning the Wikipedia community conventions of article organization:

> The advice that I received from [the Wikipedia ambassador] was very helpful in editing my article. She gave me more feedback than expected, mainly dealing with the organization of my article. I think it is very beneficial to have articles reviewed by experienced Wikipedians who know the guidelines and restrictions. After receiving [the ambassador's] advice, I was able to polish my page to make it better suited for Wikipedia.

While Wikipedia articles are never truly "finished," Mark's revisions based on the feedback received from the ambassador represent his final work on the project; and soon after, he "published" those revisions as his final draft of the assignment on Wikipedia.

As becomes evident in a case study of Mark, students working on this project benefit immensely from a cross-disciplinary digital model that invites multiple collaborators into the process. Students are challenged and motivated by the opportunity to work with different individuals, each having a separate agenda and interest in the project. The curator, for instance, is interested in sharing knowledge about a particular part of the archives as well as promoting and making archival materials more accessible through a public venue such as Wikipedia. The curator, however, doesn't always have a thorough understanding of conventional practices and politics of Wikipedia. Ambassadors working with students on this project met this need by helping students translate their research into article edits that were consistent with the encyclopedia's norms. Involving these figures in an assignment not only allows for added support and motivation for students working on a very public writing assignment—one with lasting consequences—but also creates a situation where students need to forward a vision and assert authority while working with those outside individuals. The next section deals with this issue of authority, and how students working on projects with multiple collaborators and audiences might learn to take on personal authority by gaining access to rhetorical knowledge.

Authorities, Audiences, and the Possibilities for Rhetorical Knowledge in Public Writing

In "Reading and Writing Without Authority," Ann M. Penrose and Cheryl Geisler study the writing and reading processes of two student writers—one a college freshman, the other a doctoral student—in order to better understand how novice and expert writers differ in their ability to assume authority over their writing. They argue that Janet, the freshman, "has difficulty assuming authority in a complex writing task because of her strong commitment to an 'information-transfer model of education'" (515). Janet's commitment to this model, perpetuated by the types of traditional writing assignments common in academic contexts, prohibits her from taking a constructivist approach. Instead of seeing other texts and authors as making knowledge claims "subject to interpretation and criticism" (515), Janet insists on a truth-finding writing process in order to compile an objective report, and refrains from assuming authority while negotiating multiple sources. In contrast, Roger, the more experienced writer, is able to acknowledge and negotiate multiple subjectivities in order to compare the various positions in the literature. Penrose and Geisler's examination of these two student-writers allows them to challenge preconceived notions of how students gain authority over their writing. "The traditional response to the problem of lack of authority," they acknowledge, "is to try to increase the domain knowledge upon which authority is supposedly founded" (516). Domain knowledge, the mastery of a set of subject-specific topics in a given field of inquiry, *does* provide writers with strategies to negotiate meaning. However, to assume that mastery of a complex writing task requires *only* domain knowledge is, according to Penrose and Geisler, an oversimplification. A writer's authority must also come from "rhetorical knowledge," an understanding of a rhetorical, constructivist model of knowledge production and the role of personal subjectivity in that process:

> We would instead argue for the role of rhetorical knowledge in the development of authority. In order for Janet to take authority in this or any other situation, she needs to believe there is authority to spare—that there is room for many voices. She needs to understand the development of knowledge as a communal and continual process. Thus an alternative to the information-transfer model would be

to insist on more interactive models of education in which a genuine rhetorical perspective is not only taught but enacted. (517)

An interactive pedagogy that allows students to participate in the ongoing rhetorical construction of knowledge proposed by Penrose and Geisler might be accomplished in a number of ways. The digital-collaborative model presented in this study, one responsive to community-engagement and service learning, represents a particularly productive response to their recommendations. As a wiki, a writing technology that allows for multiple, ongoing contributions to a single written product, Wikipedia itself is a productive metaphor for understanding the social construction of knowledge. Yet students also have much to gain through their negotiation of the multiple authorities and audiences afforded in a cross-disciplinary, public writing project. The involvement of these extra-academic authorities and audiences, as the results of this study suggest, allow for a pedagogy that significantly displaces the instructor as sole authority over student work and provides public audiences for student writing. Such a shift dramatically increases opportunities for growth in rhetorical knowledge, as students negotiate multiple subjectivities to produce written work for users of Wikipedia.

Table 1. Student Perceptions of Authority Distribution

Authority Figure	n (N)	%
Professor	8 (16)	50%
Wikipedia Public	8 (16)	50%
Student (Self)	6 (16)	38%
Curator	4 (16)	25%

Table 1, which presents survey data (see Appendix B, question 7), displays student perceptions of authority figures operating in the project. As is evident from the percentages, many students identified two figures of authority. While a large portion of students (8 of 16) depicted the instructor as the most significant authority—often citing the "grade" as reasoning—this selection does not represent a majority. Rather, authority was displaced among the various audiences and research partners of the assignment. An equal portion of students (8 of 16) described Wikipedia ambassadors or Wikipedia public audiences as authorities. Students in this category often reported a desire for their work to remain public on the encyclopedia (i.e., for their work not be removed by another editor). As one student responded, "I believe the Wikipedia public held the most authority because at any moment they could say your article was crap and go in and change it. This pushed me to write a better article that was constructed really well."

Additionally, a sizable portion of students (6 of 16) saw *themselves* as authorities in the project. Many of them discussed their "control" over the project, citing the public audience as a major factor:

> I held the authority, even with an online ambassador helping me and [offering] guidelines to follow. It is all my decision on what the page would consist of and how professional it would be. I cared about the assignment so I wanted to make sure that everything looks as good as possible for readers and for general public.

Finally, a smaller number of students (4 of 16) identified the special collections curator they worked with as an authority. While student perceptions are necessarily somewhat limited, these data demonstrate the possibility of displacing the instructor's authority in a public writing assignment, of enabling students to navigate multiple resources and authorities and, more importantly, cultivate their own authority in order to create knowledge in a public venue.

Much like their perceptions of authority, student conceptions of audience in this particular writing task varied greatly from a more traditional assignment in which they write for an imagined academic audience or for the instructor exclusively. Such conceptions were certainly influenced by the number of different individuals and communities involved in the project. Curators at the university library's special collections provided access to topics and materials and helped to guide students in the research process. Online Wikipedia ambassadors commented on student drafts of article edits. Students discussed their work in class among their peers, which constituted another audience. And always present: the eye of the instructor and the looming assessment. Add to these specific audiences the Wikipedia public, encyclopedia users who would read the articles, and what emerges is quite complex. Toby Coley, writing about wikis in general, provides a vivid description of such complexity:

> The concept of audience is challenged in the wiki because students now have to consider the identity of the audience on a much larger scale, since they have the ability to "publish" materials online. Though this audience may be limited by administrators, the students' conceptions of audience are still challenged through the immediacy of the audience and its impact on the physical (or digital) text. The audience is now an amalgamation of single-member audience, limited audience, undefined multi-audiences, fictionalized au-

dience, addressed, and invoked audience. ("Wikis and the Rhetorical Audience," para. 13)

Coley is drawing from Lunsford and Ede's influential 1984 work "Audience Addressed / Audience Invoked," but also relevant here is Keith Grant-Davie's identification of the audience as co-negotiating discourse with the rhetor "to achieve the rhetorical objectives" (268). For students to be able to perform such negotiations, for them to see how discourse both affects and is affected by audiences, they need to be writing for audiences beyond the instructor. A model of public writing with specific goals for production and distribution, one that involves multiple audiences and collaborators, allows for this.

When asked to identify the audience that "mattered the most to you as a writer" in the assignment sequence, students participating in the study overwhelming chose an outside audience.

Table 2. Student Identifications of Significant Audiences

n (N)	%	Identified Audience
9 (16)	56%	Wikipedia public
6 (16)	38%	Wikipedia Ambassador
3 (16)	19%	Curator
3 (16)	19%	Professor

While some students selected two audiences, which accounts for the skewing of percentages, the majority of students (9 of 16) selected the "Wikipedia public," often citing specific expectations from this audience: "The Wikipedia public mattered to me the most. I tried to put myself in someone else's shoes and think 'if I was researching the topic, what are the key things I would want to take away from it and what would I find most interesting?' With these points in mind, I put together my article."

Another large portion (6 of 16) chose the "Wikipedia Ambassador," often pointing to their expertise in the discourse community and the required processes of the assignment: "The ambassador's opinion would probably mean the most. He is supposed to be knowledgeable in the area of writing Wikipedia articles and their format. It also dictated how much more work was to be put into the project. If he didn't like it I would have to change more of the writing." Finally, an even number of students (3 of 16) chose either the curator or professor as important audiences, citing either the curator's expertise in the subject area or my final assessment as reasoning.

Interestingly, by prioritizing the professor as authority but not as audience, students overall perceived a real difference in what makes a piece of writing successful in a specific discourse community and effective in a class. Furthermore, and perhaps the most striking finding in this data, students *did* largely see themselves as writing for outside audiences. Such a finding suggests that despite the omnipresent threat of assessment and professor-authority, we can create curricula that allow students to negotiate among audiences outside the classroom and enact a pedagogy that supports students' development of rhetorical knowledge.

Factors of Motivation

The presence of extra-academic audiences provides more than an opportunity for students to gain rhetorical knowledge through negotiation of meaning with alternate groups and individuals: it also serves as a strong motivator. How do students perceive a model of cross-disciplinary digital pedagogy in comparison to previous composition assignments? Because they were students in a junior-level composition course (the second in a two-course general education requirement), participants in the study brought with them a range of experiences and opinions concerning previous exposure to composition pedagogy. Table 3 details student responses to the following prompt: "Compare this assignment to an assignment in a previous English course. Were you more or less motivated? Why?"

Table 3. Self-Assessed Student Motivation

n (N)	Motivation Level	Reasoning/Motivator
6 (16)	"More motivated"	Public/audience
4 (16)	"More motivated"	Research process/curator involvement
3 (16)	"More motivated"	New, different, unknown project
3 (16)	"More motivated"	Personal connection to topic
1 (16)	"More motivated"	Familiarity with Wikipedia
1 (16)	"Equal motivation"	Grade

Significantly, no student reported being less motivated and only one reported feeling "equal motivation." The majority of students were "more motivated" for a variety of reasons. Chief among these (6 of 16 students) was the public audience targeted by the assignment. Students were extremely motivated by the idea of publishing their work on Wikipedia. "The fact that I was working on a Wikipedia page," wrote one student, "was also more fun than just writing down facts on paper for my professor to see. It's cool that it's in [the] public domain and that helped motivate me." Others compared this larger audience to the limited audience they had written for in previous writing classes: "This was different in that I have never had an assignment that would be open to public viewing in an English class. All of my previous assignments were only read by the instructors and my classmates. This added motivation, knowing of the audience that would be reading my work."

While the public audience plays a large part in motivation, one-fourth of the students were also motivated by the research process and curator involvement in the project:

> At first I was scared of the workload. How to balance between classes, but once I got into the library I knew this was something I was going to enjoy. The researching aspect was definitely my favorite. I had never before been in the University archives, so that experience was awesome. Not only did I research for my own topic, but also went in and researched my true passion: photography. The curators even let me scan an old photo and create a poster of it to hang in my room. They were amazing which pushed me to do my best.

Yet another significant portion of students (3 of 16) were motivated by the "new" and "different" assignment model: "I believe this project motivated me because it is interesting and different. I have [been] told that using Wikipedia as a source for research was banned for such a long time. I never thought that I would be creating an article myself." An equal number of students were motivated by the opportunity to write on a topic they had a personal interest in. Finally, a smaller number of students were motivated by the opportunity to gain familiarity with Wikipedia processes and conventions and by the grade they would receive for the assignment.

Student Recommendations

While the data previously discussed demonstrates that students felt more motivation in this project as compared to previous writing assignments, this study is also concerned with answering a more specific question: would students working on this kind of cross-disciplinary, digital assignment recommend a similar model to future classes? Survey results regarding this question found that students participating in this study unanimously (16 of 16) recommend the assignment, but not all for the same reasons. As might be expected, students spoke highly of the dynamic nature of Wikipedia as a writing forum open to the public to "read, revise, and edit." Additionally, a good number of students saw this as a publishing opportunity: "Because of this project . . . I can brag to my friends that I am now a published author. This gives me great satisfaction." Students also commended the assignment for being different from writing tasks they had completed in the past, one participant calling it a "breath of fresh air compared to typical research papers that every other class is doing." Others recognized the value of multiple audiences beyond the instructor and valued gaining knowledge of the library's special collections. Finally, students also recognized the project as challenging and requiring them to "go outside [their] comfort zone." A few students, however, did have some reservations. The project would not be easy for students wanting to "slack off and write easy papers" and some stated that more time and guidance would have been helpful. Such reservations were couched in positive terms, however, and overall students expressed satisfaction with the project.

What We Can Gain

While this pilot study is certainly limited by its small sample size and lack of control group, there is much to gain from a close examination of a model of cross-disciplinary digital pedagogy. From the perspective of university libraries, and specifically special collections, this type of project accomplishes significant goals of mainstreaming and raising awareness of library archives and special collections.[2] The use of special collections is mainstreamed, in that students see this type of research as available to them in the search for information: student-participants who carried out this assignment are now more likely to utilize resources in special collections for future research endeavors and more likely to spread an awareness of archival resources among their peers. Further, awareness of the university's special collections is also cultivated for the public, as other users of Wikipedia are exposed to references and external links used in student-edited encyclopedia articles. The assignment also provides an opportunity for students to develop relationships with special collections curators. Finally, the use of Wikipedia in a cross-disciplinary writing assignment exposes librarians and curators to the numerous opportunities presented by the encyclopedia as a new model for information literacy. The importance of this collaborative model has only recently been recognized by academic librarians, as is evidenced in a recent study by Norah Bente Ismail et al.: "Few have realized the opportunities for cross-disciplinary relationships and pedagogy offered by the online encyclopedia as an alternative and more democratic episteme which might provide librarians an opportunity to engage in public intellectual tasks" (63). The curricular model offered in this study, then, is a manifestation of such opportunities, one in which librarians can engage in discourses outside their institutions as much as students.

From the perspective of the writing classroom, students also have much to gain from this model. Because it required local archival research and the translation of that research into a publicly accessible forum online, the collaborative, cross-disciplinary conditions of the project allowed students to both participate in and observe the ways in which digital technologies are changing how information is produced, shared and accessed in the twenty-first century. Opportunities for the displacement of authority figures and the negotiation of multiple audiences make the enactment of rhetorical knowledge and the assertion of student authority a viable option in the composition classroom. Furthermore, as realized by scholars studying the convergences of Wikipedia and writing pedagogy, students exposed to the acts of composing that take place on the online encyclopedia can gain an understanding of writing as a recursive, collaborative, and utterly social process (Hood; Purdy; Vetter). That student-participants in this study unanimously recommended the assignment model further demonstrates their perception of its value.

Ultimately, coming to more concrete realizations of the opportunities provided by digital pedagogies and their implementation into service-learning environments also answers calls from Adler-Kassner, Crooks, and Watters to identify more sustainable ways to promote and position service-learning in the academy. Forging cross-disciplinary relationships with university archives and special collections and working together to contribute to a digital public knowledge project such as Wikipedia helps us reimagine the notion of the archive in light of recent and rapid technological change. Etymologically speaking, *archive* connotes the collection and storage of public records, yet the word is also linked to definitions of authority and power. *Archive* shares a morpheme with cognates *monarchy* and *oligarchy*, and is, in its most basic form, evocative of the power of the state to regulate public knowledge. Reconfiguring the archive in the twenty-first century, and harnessing digital technologies that are themselves more democratic, serves librarians and students in very positive ways while also demonstrating what public writing pedagogies can accomplish outside the academy.

Appendix A: Project Assignments

Process Log Prompt 1

After writing the proposal and meeting with your curator, describe this part of the project's influence on your progress. How has it affected the writing you've completed thus far on the project?

Process Log Prompt 2

After posting to your online ambassador's page and gaining their feedback, what have you learned about how a writer's audience can influence his or her writing? How has your interaction with the online ambassador influenced your writing?

Curator Proposal Letter Assignment

In "What Is It We Do When We Write Articles Like This One—and How Can We Get Students to Joins Us?," Michael Kleine relates the knowledge he gains from interviewing eight professors about their writing processes. Among his findings, Kleine highlights the emphasis these professional writers place on their "involvement in genuine research communities" which serve as "starting points" for their own work (27). What we can learn from Kleine is that successful writing is always social and always requires input from and dialogue with other writers and thinkers who are involved in a community in which you are both members.

For this assignment, you'll initiate a conversation by contacting the curator who works in your topic area in order to gain valuable feedback about your proposed Wikipedia project. These curators are, in a sense, part of a community we've created that has a shared goal: to enable effective and valuable contributions to Wikipedia articles.

To accomplish this, you'll write a letter to the curator, utilizing the conventions of the genre of a letter (salutation and closing). Your letter should be 700–900 words and should be emailed to your assigned curator. Each email should also be cc'd to the instructor. As you write, be sure to address the following:

- Thank the curator for their involvement in your writing process.
- Identify a gap in the article, sections which could be expanded or corrected/updated. If creating a new article, explain why such an article is worthwhile and what information you might need and have already found to warrant its creation.
- Discuss how you can fill this gap with research you've already done at the special collections and archives.
- Provide an outline of your proposed edits/additions or your new article.
- Ask the curator for help with additional research problems/questions.
- Confirm your interview time.

Appendix B: Survey

Student Survey Questions

1. How did having multiple audiences for this assignment (your peers, the teacher, curators, Wikipedia ambassadors, other Wikipedia users who might view your article) change the writing you did on this project?

2. What about those audiences who were outside the classroom (curators, Wikipedia public, ambassadors) more specifically? How did your awareness of them in particular affect your approach to the assignment?
3. Over the course of the entire project, which of these audiences seemed to matter the most to you as a writer?
4. In your opinion, your success on this project depended mostly on your ability to meet the expectations of which audience or audiences? Why do you think that is?
5. Compare this writing assignment to an assignment in a previous English course. Were you more or less motivated? Why?
6. Think about how a teacher's authority and expertise (on the form and subject of your writing) normally influences a writing assignment. How was authority in this project distributed (or not) among audiences?
7. Who held the most authority for this project? And how has this influenced your writing?
8. Would you recommend this assignment to a future class? Why or why not?

Notes

1. Such a conceptualization departs from Henry Giroux's use of the term to describe the political and educational effects of mass media and global culture.

2. For a discussion of how this project achieved the goals of special collections and archives at Ohio University Libraries, see Matthew Vetter and Sarah Harrington, "Integrating Special Collections into the Composition Classroom: A Case Study of Collaborative Digital Curriculum."

Works Cited

Adler-Kassner, Linda, Robert Crooks, and Ann Watters. *Writing the Community: Concepts and Models for Service-Learning in Composition*. Washington, DC: Amer. Assoc. for Higher Educ., 1997. Print.

Barton, Matthew D. "The Future of Rational-Critical Debate in Online Public Spheres." *Computers and Composition* 22.2 (2005): 177-90. Print.

Bizzell, Patricia. *Academic Discourse and Critical Consciousness*. Pittsburgh: U of Pittsburgh P, 1992. Print.

Boyatzis, Richard E. *Transforming Qualitative Information: Thematic Analysis and Code Development*. Thousand Oaks: Sage, 1998. Print.

Bruffee, Kenneth A. "Collaborative Learning and the 'Conversation of Mankind.'" *College English* 46.7 (1984): 635-52. Print.

Coley, Toby. "Through the Looking Monitor: Alice in Wikiland." *Computers and Composition Online* (Spring 2011): n. pag. Web. 11 Mar. 2012.

Deans, Thomas. *Writing Partnerships: Service-learning in Composition*. Urbana: NCTE, 2000. Print.

Ede, Lisa, and Andrea Lunsford. "Audience Addressed/Audience Invoked: The Role of Audience in Composition Theory and Pedagogy." *CCC* 35.2 (1984): 155-71. Print.

Feldman, Ann M. *Making Writing Matter: Composition in the Engaged University.* Albany: SUNY, 2008. Print.

Gee, James P. "Literacy, Discourse, and Linguistics: Introduction." *Journal of Education* 171.1 (1989): 5-17. Print.

Giroux, Henry. "Cultural Studies, Public Pedagogy, and the Responsibility of Intellectuals." *Communication and Critical/Cultural Studies* 1.1 (2004): 59-79. Print.

Grant-Davie, Keith. "Rhetorical Situations and Their Constituents." *Rhetoric Review* 15.2 (1997): 264-79. Print.

Harris, Joseph. "The Idea of Community in the Study of Writing." *CCC* 40.1 (1989): 11-22. Print.

Herzberg, Bruce. "Community Service and Critical Teaching." *CCC* 45.3 (1994): 307-19. Print.

Hood, Carra Leah. "Editing Out Obscenity: Wikipedia and Writing Pedagogy." *Computers and Composition Online* (Spring 2009): n. pag. Web. 11 Mar. 2012.

Ismail, Norah Binte, et al. "Librarian Perception of Wikipedia: Threats Or Opportunities for Librarianship?" *Libri: International Journal of Libraries & Information Services* 60.1 (2010): 57-64. Print.

Jarratt, Susan C. *Rereading the Sophists: Classical Rhetoric Refigured.* Carbondale, IL: SIUP, 1991. Print.

Kleine, Michael. "What Is It We Do When We Write Articles Like This One— and How Can We Get Students to Joins Us?" *Writing About Writing: A College Reader.* Eds. Elizabeth Wardle and Doug Downs. Boston: Bedford/St. Martin's, 2011. 22-32. Print.

Penrose, Ann M., and Cheryl Geisler. "Reading and Writing without Authority." *CCC* 45.4 (1994): 505-20. Print.

Purdy, James P. "When the Tenets of Composition Go Public: A Study of Writing in Wikipedia." *CCC* 61.2 (2009): 351-71. Print.

Richards, Daniel. "Digitizing Dewey: Blogging an Ethic of Community." *Computers and Composition Online* (Fall 2011): n. pag. Web. 11 Mar. 2012.

Vetter, Matthew. "Composing with Wikipedia: A Classroom Study of Online Writing." *Computers and Composition Online* (Winter 2013): n. pag. Web. 10 Feb. 2013.

Vetter, Matthew, and Sarah Harrington. "Integrating Special Collections into the Composition Classroom: A Case Study of Collaborative Digital Curriculum." *Research Library Issues* 283 (2013). Web. 22 Jan. 2014.

Weisser, Christian R. *Moving Beyond Academic Discourse: Composition Studies and the Public Sphere.* Carbondale, IL: SIUP, 2002. Print.

"Wikipedia: Education Program." *Wikipedia, The Free Encyclopedia.* Wikimedia Foundation. 22 Sept. 2013. Web. 30 Jan. 2014.

Instruction, Cognitive Scaffolding, and Motivational Scaffolding in Writing Center Tutoring

Jo Mackiewicz and Isabelle Thompson

In this study, we quantitatively analyze the discourse of experienced writing center tutors in 10 highly satisfactory conferences. Specifically, we analyze tutors' instruction, cognitive scaffolding, and motivational scaffolding, all tutoring strategies identified in prior research from other disciplines as educationally effective. We find that tutors used the instructional strategies of telling and suggesting, the cognitive scaffolding strategy of pumping, and the motivational scaffolding strategy of showing concern most frequently. We argue that the interdisciplinary analytical framework that we developed and describe in this article can facilitate further analysis of tutors' talk and thus help move research beyond the local level of the individual writing center. Finally, we point to some ways that our findings can inform tutor training.

As Stephen North once wrote and as any tutor knows, in writing center conferences, "talk is everything" (75). However, even though writing center research has progressed substantially since North's famous statement first appeared in 1984, as Michael Pemberton points out, very little empirical research describing writing center talk has been conducted. Over the past few years, the two of us have tried to help fill this gap in the research (see Mackiewicz and Thompson; Thompson; Thompson and Mackiewicz). Here, we report on our third coauthored and most comprehensive study, a quantitative analysis of tutoring strategies identified through research conducted in other disciplines as educationally effective. Our research differs from most quantitative studies of writing center discourse in that we limited our analysis to conferences that trained, experienced tutors conducted and that students and tutors rated as far above average or highly satisfactory. Therefore, instead of attempting to describe issues such as gender or power by coding a random selection of conferences, we selected the 10 highest-rated conferences from our existing corpus of 51 writing center conferences to identify what arguably good tutors—at least in one writing center—did in their attempt to provide educational opportunities for students.

In this article we extend our previous discussions of cognitive and motivational scaffolding, as well as describe in detail the more explicitly directive tutoring strategy of instruction. Defined generally, scaffolding metaphorically refers to a learning opportunity in which a more expert tutor teaches a less expert student to answer a question, correct an error, or perform a task without telling the student the answer or doing the work for him or her. The tutor acts as a scaffold, helping the student to do things he or she cannot perform alone. Instruction refers to the directive aspects of tutoring—supplying solutions or options rather than supporting or making room for students to generate solutions themselves. Our goals for this article are the following: (1) to present the framework—the coding scheme—that we developed, a scheme that we believe can facilitate further study of tutors' talk and thus help move research beyond the local level of the individual writing center; (2) to comprehensively describe and analyze 10 experienced tutors' strategies in satisfactory conferences, (3) to point to some ways that our findings can inform tutor training.

Rebecca Day Babcock, Kellye Manning, and Travis Rogers have suggested that the notion of scaffolding, stemming from the work of educational psychologists David Wood, Jerome S. Bruner, and Gail Ross, is important for understanding what experienced tutors say and do in writing center conferences to support student writers' improvement. However, few published empirical studies exist that examine scaffolding. Most research about scaffolding examines problem-solving disciplines such as math (Putnam) and physics (Chi), readily describable tasks such as decoding in adult literacy instruction (Cromley and Azevedo), and the use of specialized computer software (Lehman et al.). Such research describes in detail the strategies that both experienced and inexperienced tutors use when working in highly structured domains. In this article and in our previous studies, we draw upon this research to analyze the tutoring strategies of experienced writing center tutors.

We began our analysis with the coding scheme that Jennifer G. Cromley and Roger Azevedo developed to examine tutor discourse, specifically, the tutoring strategies that experienced and inexperienced tutors used to teach decoding skills to adult literacy students. Cromley and Azevedo developed their coding scheme from previous studies examining instruction and scaffolding in tutoring sessions. We chose their scheme for classifying tutoring strategies as the basis for our own because of its foundation in studies of tutoring and because it describes tutoring strategies in detail. However, the well-structured task of decoding, like math (Putnam) and physics (Chi) problem solving and software procedures (Lehman et al.), is a closed-world domain task, where "[t]he questions and answers typically are well-defined . . . and one can distinguish between good and bad answers" (Person et al. 185). In contrast, problem solving in writing, an open-world domain like many other humanistic and social science fields, is less concerned with single correct answers or predictable strategic moves than with often nebulous notions of effectiveness defined loosely by audience, purpose, and other incredibly variable rhetorical considerations. No coding scheme for tutoring strategies had yet been developed for tutoring open-world domains such as writing, so we modified Cromley and Azevedo's detailed scheme to make it useful for studying the talk of writing center conferences.

As we discuss in further detail below, we augmented Cromley and Azevedo's scheme with Penelope Brown and Stephen C. Levinson's politeness theory and with Bruner and his associates' work on motivation and revised the scheme's categories based on recursive review of our discourse data and retrospective interviews with tutors. In its final version, our scheme allowed us to classify tutors' verbal strategies according to Cromley and Azevedo's three broad categories: instruction, where tutors do not scaffold but instead tell students what to do and explain answers; cognitive scaffolding, where tutors give students opportunities to figure out what to do on their own; and motivational scaffolding, where tutors provide encouragement. We applied the coding scheme to the 10 highest-rated conferences in our corpus of 51 previously video recorded and transcribed conferences and determined the frequency of tutoring strategies across the three categories. That analysis led us to describe each category in more detail. We found that tutors used instruction more often than scaffolding but that instruction in the open-world domain of writing is much more demanding than simply telling a student what to do. In fact, like cognitive scaffolding, instruction can open up writing's complexity even as it provides some boundaries to direct students' thinking.

A Brief Recap of Scaffolding

Bruner and his associates in cognitive psychology coined the term "scaffolding" in the mid-1970s. Reporting their observations of young children building block towers with help from an adult tutor, Wood, Bruner, and Ross discuss scaffolding as a "process that enables the child or novice to solve a problem, carry out a task, or achieve a goal which would be beyond his unassisted efforts" (90). They describe the tutor's responsibilities in the scaffolding process as recruiting the child's interest and maintaining his or her focus on building the tower, helping the child avoid and correct errors, simplifying the child's role in completing the task, keeping the child from becoming frustrated and anxious during work on the task, and modeling and explaining to allow the child to imitate the adult's expert strategies. In scaffolding, therefore, tutors concern themselves with motivation along with skill development.

As the educational psychology research of David Wood and David Middleton showed, scaffolding moves learners along in their thinking and their learning. Rather than studying tutors, Wood and Middleton observed mothers teaching their children how to build the same block tower. They concluded that mothers who based their teaching on their children's most recent responses and who concentrated their teaching within their children's "region of sensitivity to instruction" were the most likely to facilitate successful outcomes (181).

Described as "a hypothetical measure of the child's current task ability and his 'readiness' for different topics" (181), the region of sensitivity to instruction has become associated with Lev Vygotsky's zone of proximal development. The tutor can determine and assess the student's region of sensitivity to instruction by actively adapting the instruction to the student's responses; the tutor's move hinges on the student's. If the student responds incorrectly or appears to lose interest or confidence, the tutor offers more support; if the student is successful and interested, the tutor moves forward until the student can complete the task alone. As the student becomes better able to regulate his or her efforts independently, control of the process moves from external (the tutor's instruction) to internal (the student's self-instruction). Finally, when the student is able to perform the task without assistance, the tutor hands it over (Tharp and Gallimore) and fades, leaving the student to take charge (Puntambekar and Hübscher; Stone). According to mathematics education researchers Derek Holton and David Clarke, scaffolding not only assists students in solving immediate problems but also helps students learn the right way to ask questions and therefore "provide the basis for independent learning" (131). One-to-one tutoring remains a dominant topic of scaffolding research, but such research has not examined the open-world domain of writing tutoring. Our study helps fill this gap.

Method

In this section we discuss our study participants and their conference sessions, as well as our procedure for recording and coding tutoring strategies.

Conferences

We selected the 10 conferences used in this IRB-approved study from a corpus of 51 conferences that we video recorded and transcribed for related research on tutoring from 2005 to 2008 at Auburn University. While the writing center where these conferences were conducted typically offered 30-minute sessions, the 10 conferences we studied ranged from 17 to 40 minutes, totaling approximately 5.5 hours. We selected these 10 because participants evaluated them as above average or as very satisfactory in postconference surveys. We determined participants' level of satisfaction via two items on the postconference survey. One question asked the conference participants to rate their perceptions of the conference success on a six-point scale (1 = not successful and 6 = very successful). Five of the 10 students rated the conferences as 6 and five as 5 in terms of success; eight of the 10 tutors rated the conferences as 6 and two as 5 in terms of success. A second question asked students to rate their intent to implement ideas and advice from the conference discussion and asked tutors to predict the extent to which they thought students would implement conference ideas and advice (1 = none and 6 = very much). Seven of the 10 students responded with 6 and three with 5; seven of the 10 tutors responded with 6 and three with 5. From these survey results, we concluded that both the 10 students and the 10 tutors were quite satisfied with their conferences.

Participants

All of the tutors were experienced, as all were in their second year or more of working in the writing center. All had completed a semester-long training practicum, and several were participating in the practicum again as assistant coordinators or as mentors for inexperienced tutors. Seven of the 10 tutors were graduate assistants teaching the courses that generated the assignments discussed in the conferences, though not the same sections in which the participating students were enrolled. The other three tutors were advanced undergraduates pursuing either English majors or English minors. All had overall GPAs of at least 3.5. The graduate students worked in the writing center without being screened, but the undergraduates had been rigorously screened—nominated by an instructor, interviewed, and required to provide a satisfactory writing sample and pass a proofreading test. Therefore, all of the tutors can be considered accomplished writers, strong students, and trained and experienced tutors. All ten tutors were non-Hispanic white. Seven tutors were female; three were male.

The 10 students in these conferences were all undergraduates enrolled in two university-required core courses, first-year writing and world literature. Two were African-American; the rest were non-Hispanic white. Three students were male; seven were female. All of the tutors and students were native speakers of American English. Certainly, such a restriction limits the applicability of our findings, and future research should include writing center conferences involving tutors and students who speak and write English as a foreign or second language, but such an analysis was beyond the scope of this project.

Procedure

To code our conferences for tutoring strategies, as noted before, we modified Cromley and Azevedo's coding scheme, refining it for writing center tutoring in three important ways. First, we differentiated between telling and suggesting strategies based on analysis of more- and less-direct language (Mackiewicz and Riley). Second, we separated as two strategy types what Cromley and Azevedo group together as hints. Our scheme identifies suggestions (i.e., direct-though-mitigated advice) and (true) hinting; therefore, it recognizes that suggestions such as "You could use a graph to present this data" offer advice (and thus are instructional strategies) and hints such as "Visuals often facilitate comprehension" prod thinking (and thus are cognitive scaffolding strategies). Such a distinction is critical for coding writing center tutoring, where tutors offer mitigated yet clear advice. Third, we augmented scaffolding research with Brown and Levinson's politeness theory and Albert Bandura's research about self-efficacy.

We determined inter-rater reliability for our scheme by coding a subset of 60 tutor turns for tutoring strategies and then calculating Cohen's kappa, a statistical test useful for determining inter-rater reliability. One of the authors and a trained graduate assistant coded the conferences for tutoring strategies. Coders separately analyzed each conference and achieved 88% agreement on their coding; then, they met to examine the coding discrepancies. They discussed the discrepancies, examining the context of each code collaboratively and coming to an agreement on the best strategy code. The Cohen's kappa statistic was 0.717, a very good level of agreement—with .40 to .75 usually considered good, and over .75 considered excellent (Landis and Koch). Finally, for most conferences, we also video recorded retrospective interviews with the tutors. We played back the video recording of each conference and asked the tutor why he or she used certain tutoring strategies. These interviews informed our interpretations of tutors' most likely intentions.

Tutoring Strategies

As previously stated, we coded and analyzed three categories of tutoring strategies: instruction, cognitive scaffolding, and motivational scaffolding. Below we offer detailed descriptions of each strategy.

Instructional Strategies

Instruction includes telling (directive, with little or no mitigation) and suggesting (directive, with much more mitigation), when advising students about necessary or potential changes in a draft, outline, plan, or even the composing process itself. It also includes tutors' telling and suggesting ways of achieving the student's agenda during a conference and post conference. When telling and suggesting, tutors sometimes use explanations or examples to help student writers implement (and possibly, for tutors to justify) their advice. Indeed, instruction can diminish students' active participation in learning opportunities, possibly because it negates students' need to arrive at and explain ideas to themselves (Chi et al., "Self-Explanations"; Chi et al., "Eliciting Self-Explanations"). When tutors use instruction and tell students what to do, they have to ensure that in receiving such directiveness students can "save face," that is, avoid embarrassment and maintain control of their writing. Brown and Levinson delineate politeness strategies that help mitigate the face threat of directive advice, called negative politeness strategies, and research on writing center talk has focused mainly on these. Negative politeness strategies, including modal verbs such as "could" and downgraders such as "maybe," "a little bit," and "just" help tutors (and others) suggest rather than tell (e.g., Mackiewicz, "The Effects," "Functions"; Thonus, "Dominance," "How to Communicate Politely"). Research on tutors' discourse has concluded that tutors' goals to be both clear and polite sometimes conflict, that politeness sometimes generates ambiguous advice (Thonus, "Dominance," "How to"), and that tutors' expertise (and, likely, the confidence it brings) may encourage the use of negative politeness strategies as well as positive politeness strategies—strategies such as praise, joking, and optimism—that signal solidarity and rapport (Mackiewicz, "The Effects" 322).

As readers of *Composition Studies* know, early advice for writing center tutors opposed directiveness, but such advice was not informed by empirical research on politeness or on instruction's impact on learning. To honor the peer relationship between tutors and students, along with the practical concern of negating teachers' worries about plagiarism (Clark and Healy), writing center tutors were to avoid usurping control of students' writing by avoiding directiveness—telling and suggesting (Ashton-Jones; Brooks). Tutors were to help students improve their composing processes, rather than tell them how to improve a particular draft or respond to a particular assignment (Harris; Healy; North). In addition, if they disregarded prevalent sentiments about "good" tutoring and turned their focus from process to product, they were to refrain from telling by drawing upon students' existing reservoirs of knowledge (i.e., by using scaffolding strategies). It is important to note that empirical research has since found that tutors mainly ignore the proscription against instruction and that students actually welcome and expect tutor directiveness, so long as they control the conference agenda (Clark; Davis et al.; Thonus, "Triangulation," "Tutor and Student Assessments"; Wolcott). Thus, writing center specialists more and more acknowledge the need for tutors, as more expert institutional representatives, to offer advice (Kiedaisch and Dinitz; Mackiewicz, "The Effects"; Shamoon and Burns; Trimbur).

In our study, instruction comprised three strategies:

- Telling: Tutors use little to no mitigation to direct students in revising or brainstorming ideas and in pointing out errors or problems (e.g., "Put it in there, at the beginning of that one."). Tutors also use little to no mitigation to direct students in improving their composing processes (e.g., "Make sure they all relate back to that thesis as well.").
- Suggesting: Tutors use more mitigation, thus lowering the face threat of their advice. They often use negative politeness (e.g., "But since the focus of the paper is law enforcement, you probably want to bring it back to law enforcement here.").

- Explaining and exemplifying: Tutors offer reasons for and illustrate their advice (e.g., "Because you're saying, you know, they cause their life to be or feel meaningless. And it seems like from what we talked about here you're going to say, like, however, in *Notes from the Underground*, the author does show that there's hope for a better life.").

Cognitive Scaffolding Strategies

Cognitive scaffolding includes strategies such as pumping questions (e.g., "What's another possibility here?") that prod and help students to think. These strategies range in the extent to which they constrain student responses (Boyer et al.; Lehman et al.). For example, a pumping question such as "What's another possibility here?" allows for a wider range of student responses than a question such as "Do you know what part of speech this is?" However, no matter the extent to which cognitive scaffolding strategies constrain students' responses, through the turn-taking "rules" of conversation, they—unlike other strategies—require responses (for example, by providing an answer to a question) (Thornbury and Slade). In prodding student responses, cognitive scaffolding strategies create opportunities for students to construct and connect ideas and to display what they do not know and understand.

A predominant form of cognitive scaffolding, pumping often occurs in the form of questions. Two such categories are information-seeking questions, also called negotiatory or open questions (Severino; Smith and Higgins), and known-information questions, also called closed, display, or leading questions (Nassaji and Wells; Piazza). Research on questions in classroom teaching has shown that the Socratic method—back-and-forth questions and answers—is a more effective teaching strategy than uninterrupted instruction (Rose et al.; see also, Kintsch; Tienken, Goldberg, and DiRocco). Along with encouraging active participation in learning (Lustick; Smith and Higgins), cognitive scaffolding (i.e., pumping) questions help students formulate explanations for themselves (Chi; Chi et al., "Eliciting Self-Explanations"; Chi et al., "Self-Explanations"; Rose et al.; Smith and Higgins). Further, tutors' questions can model effective questioning and thus can help students develop self-scaffolding strategies.

In a recent study of writing center talk, we identified and classified tutors' questions in 11 conferences (Thompson and Mackiewicz). We found that 33.6% of tutors' 690 questions were known-information questions. In contrast, only 8.7% were genuine information-seeking questions. Another 33.5% were motivational scaffolding questions that showed the tutors' concern for students' understanding and ownership (e.g., "Does that make sense?"). We found that tutors sometimes moved from known-information to information-seeking questions, giving a student an opportunity to take control after pointing the student in a potentially successful direction.

Eight tutoring strategies composed our cognitive scaffolding category:

- Pumping: Tutors withhold their advice or part of the answer. Pumping can be constraining (e.g., "Where does the comma go in this sentence?") or open ended (e.g., "What does the poem mean to you?"). We included leading questions in this category because they can act as pumps for thinking and require at least minimal responses from students (e.g., "Isn't this change in topic a good spot for a paragraph break?").

- Reading aloud: Tutors read sections of students' drafts aloud so that students can hear what they have written. In addition, tutors read teachers' assignment sheets aloud to help students understand the writing requirements better and to model the sort of word-by-word attention to detail required for understanding assignments. For example, a tutor might read aloud the gist of the assignment from the instructor's explanatory handout (e.g., "You must state your position on an issue and convince your reader that your position is correct."). Tutors also ask students to read their drafts aloud to identify errors and passages that need revision and to teach students a strategy they may use after they leave the writing center.

- Responding as a reader: Tutors read a section from a draft, either aloud or silently, and then tell students what they take away as readers. They paraphrase what they think students are saying in order to help them compare tutors' paraphrases with their intended meaning (e.g., "You say that, you know, this is the way I like it because it's suitable to my needs in getting things done.").

- Referring to a previous topic: When tutors see that students are making the same error or having the same problem in several places in a draft, they refer the students back to the earlier occurrence to help them identify the problem and practice the previously discussed revision or correction strategy (e.g., "And then, T-O-O, 'too good.' Again, like we talked about in the beginning.").

- Forcing a choice: Tutors present students with several alternatives, one of which is correct, and expect students to choose the correct alternative. Forcing a choice constrains, and therefore directs, students' responses to increase their chances of success (e.g., "Now, 'the boys tell their friends,' or 'the boys tells their friends'?").

- Prompting, hinting, and demonstrating: These strategies rarely occurred in our writing center data (see Chi for further discussion of these strategies in closed-world domain tutoring).

Motivational Scaffolding Strategies

Intertwined with both cognition and affect, motivation influences students' effort, persistence (Bransford, Brown, and Cocking), and their active participation and engagement in the conference (Evens and Michael). Motivation influences and is influenced by students' interest in the tasks they are performing, their self-efficacy in successfully completing those tasks, and their ability to self-regulate their performances (Hidi and Boscolo; see DeCheck for a discussion of motivation in writing center tutoring based on a slightly different theoretical perspective). Individual interest, associated with intrinsic motivation, is likely to increase learning both within and beyond the tutorial conference (Bye, Pushkar, and Conway; Lepper and Henderlong). Self-efficacy (Bandura; Pajares and Valiante; Shell, Murphy, and Bruning) and self-regulation (Zimmerman; Zimmerman and Kitsantas; Zimmerman and Schunk) are mutually dependent, with self-efficacy (roughly analogous to self-confidence) known to influence effort, persistence, and activity choice and with self-regulation relating to organizing a task and managing task completion, including finding help if needed. In short, by increasing students' interest, self-efficacy, and self-regulation, motivational scaffolding has the potential to make an impact on students' learning.

Tutors can enhance students' motivation by helping them feel comfortable and supported (Bruning and Horn) and can build, even in a short time, feelings of rapport and solidarity through certain politeness strategies, particularly positive politeness strategies (Brown and Levinson). The strategies we categorize as motivational scaffolding provide encouragement in a variety of ways.

Studies of positive politeness in writing center conferences are less common than studies of negative politeness. However, one study found that tutors use the plural pronoun "we" to include both conversation participants in the activity (Murphy). Another study showed that when working with the same student over a six-week period, some tutors increasingly relied on positive politeness, such as inclusive language and praise (Bell, Arnold, and Haddock), likely because they had built a measure of rapport. Other research has suggested that students' perceptions of their comfort during conferences strongly correlate with their overall conference satisfaction (Thompson et al.; Thonus, "Tutor and Student Assessments") and with their willingness to return for future conferences (Carino and Enders).

Our scheme captures five types of motivational scaffolding:

- Showing concern: Tutors build rapport with students by demonstrating that they care. Such demonstrations of concern can be formulaic, as when a tutor asks about a student's understanding with a collocation (e.g., "Does that make sense?") or nonformulaic, as when a tutor attends to a student's emotional well-being (e.g., "You're feeling less overwhelmed now that you've found it's not hard at all?").
- Praising: Tutors point to students' successes with positive feedback and verbal rewards. Praise, too, can be formulaic (e.g., "That's good.") and nonformulaic (e.g., "I think it has a subtlety to it, which is . . . very nice. And I think that's a difficult thing for lots of students to achieve in their writing.").
- Reinforcing students' ownership and control: Tutors increase students' developing self-regulation and self-efficacy by asserting that the student ultimately makes the decisions (e.g., "Well, I mean . . . that's something that is ultimately up to you.").
- Using humor and being optimistic: Tutors reduce students' anxiety with light-heartedness and build confidence by asserting a student's ability to persevere in the task. (For example, a tutor used self-deprecating humor when jotting down a note: "Uh, consequences for your actions. Wrong and right. Whatever. I can't spell consequences.").
- Giving sympathy and empathy: Tutors express their understanding that the task is difficult (e.g., "And it's a difficult thing to analyze senses.").

Overall Results

We calculated the frequency with which tutors used the tutoring strategies in the instruction, cognitive scaffolding, and motivational scaffolding categories. Tutors used 31.16 strategies each 10 minutes of interaction—or, just over 3 strategies per minute. Clearly, the tutors in these successful conferences saturated their sessions with strategies and moved among the three types of strategies. But of the three strategies, tutors used instruction far more often than either cognitive or motivational scaffolding: in fact, instruction occurred on average 13.86 times per 10 minutes. Nearly half (45%) of tutors' total tutoring strategies fell into the instruction category. This finding suggests that tutors saw or sensed the utility in telling, suggesting, and explaining and exemplifying what students should do. In contrast, tutors used an average of 10.54 cognitive scaffolding (34%) and 6.76 motivational scaffolding (22%) strategies each 10 minutes. Table 1 shows the frequency distribution across the three categories.

Table 1. Frequency and Percentage of Tutoring Strategies per 10 Minutes.

Tutoring Strategy Category	Frequency	Frequency per 10 Minutes (% Total)
Instruction	438	13.86 (45)
Cognitive scaffolding	326	10.54 (34)
Motivational scaffolding	214	6.76 (22)
Total	978	31.16 (100)

Another main finding from this study was that tutors used four strategies from across the three categories far more frequently than the other types: telling (instruction), pumping (cognitive scaffolding), suggesting (instruction), and showing concern (motivational scaffolding). Table 2 shows the frequencies and percentages; it reveals that tutors used about the same percentage of pumps and suggestions (each comprising 18% of tutors' total strategies).

Table 2. Frequency and Percentage of Tutors' Most-Frequent Strategies.

Tutoring Strategy Type	Category	Frequency per 10 Minutes (% Total)
Telling	Instruction	5.97 (19)
Pumping	Cognitive scaffolding	5.91 (18)
Suggesting	Instruction	5.68 (18)
Showing concern	Motivational scaffolding	3.32 (11)
Other strategies	All categories	10.28 (34)
Total		31.16 (100)

As Table 2 shows, tutors were directive in telling and in offering suggestions about what to do, but they balanced that instruction with cognitive scaffolding attempts to get students to consider and reconsider the content, form, and process of their writing, as well as with encouragement—signals that they cared about students' comprehension and well-being (motivational scaffolding). With these four most-frequent strategies, the tutors varied their pedagogical approaches to create conferences that both they and their student clients considered successful.

Instruction: Close Analysis

Tutors used telling and suggesting to relate targeted advice about what students should or could do to improve their drafts or make their composing processes more efficient.

Table 3 breaks down the frequency with which tutors used telling, suggesting, and explaining instructional strategies. (Exemplifying strategies were very rare.) The tutors employed the instructional strategies of telling and suggesting with about equal frequency per 10 minutes but typically did not provide the related explanations and examples. Based on early practitioner advice, the tutors should have avoided telling and suggesting strategies, practicing what Brooks and others call nondirective tutoring. Instead, like Terese Thonus ("Tutor"), we found that tutors advised students on their draft papers, the assignments students brought with them, as well as the writing process.

Table 3. Frequencies and Percentage of Instruction Strategies per 10 Minutes.

Instruction Type	Example	Frequency per 10 Minutes (% Total)
Telling	"Try to take that 'it' out."	5.97 (43)
Suggesting	"But since the focus of the paper is law enforcement, you probably want to bring it back to law enforcement here."	5.68 (41)
Explaining	"Because see, something like this. This is kind of an example. Right here where you say 'I was not used to sitting with girls at lunch anyway.' That's a reference to your private to your public school."	2.21 (16)
Total		13.86 (100)

By telling rather than suggesting, tutors risked imposing their views on students. Perhaps these experienced tutors believed that their institutionally superior role and their greater expertise obligated them to dispense advice as unambiguously as possible. Even the undergraduate tutors—who had never assumed the institutionally defined role of "teacher" and were closer in age to the student writers—did not hesitate to use telling instructional strategies. But, as noted before, the students had rated the conferences highly, suggesting that they took no offence to tutors' instruction and may even have preferred the unambiguous advice.

Based on the difficulty of and the amount of time required for students to enact their advice, we surmise that tutors provided instruction intended for after the conference. That is, tutors expected students to think through both major and, in many cases, sentence-level revisions on their own. Although Thonus

("Dominance") distinguishes between advice that tutors expect students to implement during conferences versus after conferences, we could not reliably distinguish between these two types: often tutors pointed out a problem (for example, misused punctuation) likely with the intent that the students should both revise immediately and also look for similar problems post conference. For example, Tutor 8 (T8) indicates with "just so you know" that she expects the student to look for other misused semicolons other than the one they have discussed and to correct them after they have finished up the conference: "OK. Just so you know, after you have a semicolon, here, this is a fragment. You need a full sentence." This distinction allows us to see how instruction—despite its controversial history in writing center scholarship—can lead to thoughtful and engaged student participation in the composing process, participation that has often gone unnoticed in studies of writing center interaction.

Because in some cases students must apply tutors' advice post conference, even at its most directive, tutors' instruction can lead to thoughtful and engaged participation in the composing process—if not during their conferences, then after. For example, T9 brainstormed with Student 9 (S9) about ways to respond to a world literature assignment:

> T9: OK. So we will call this A. Well, A is obviously going to be your thesis, but I would not really try to start the thesis especially in this type of a paper. Don't write your thesis until you've written your paper. Because it is kind of an exploratory paper, and he [the instructor] does kind of say, you know, um . . . where did it go? [Referring to the assignment sheet.] Oh yeah, "The debatable question to be explored." Since it is exploratory, just start writing the paper and then go back and write your thesis.

Several times, T9 told the student what to do ("I would not really try to start the thesis ..." and "Don't write your thesis until you've written your paper"). She also explained her advice ("Because it is kind of an exploratory paper..."). With this instruction, T9 provided composing strategies that S9 could apply to future writing assignments.

Cognitive Scaffolding: Close Analysis

One of the hallmarks of one-to-one tutoring across all disciplines is the opportunity to move away from instruction to a more Socratic teaching style that is difficult to practice in the classroom. Cognitive scaffolding probes students' thinking and gets them to answer questions or perform tasks they cannot perform without scaffolding support. Table 4 shows that tutors used pumping more often than any other cognitive scaffolding strategy. In fact, they used it more often than all of the other cognitive scaffolding strategies combined.

Table 4. Frequency and Percentage of Cognitive Scaffolding per 10 Minutes.

Cognitive Scaffold Type	Example	Frequency per 10 Minutes (% Total)
Pumping	"So why, why do you think it's, it's effective?"	5.91 (55)
Reading aloud	[Reading from the student's paper.] "'The estimated total number of people living in the U.S. with a viral STD is over 65 million. At least 25 percent of them were teenagers.'"	2.18 (23)
Responding as reader	"I mean, this paragraph is saying any case. But you're specifically saying in the case of law enforcement."	1.27 (11)
Referring to a previous topic	"Well, that the absurdity in itself is that, like, I mean what you said in the very beginning."	0.54 (5)
Forcing a choice	"Would it be easier for you to talk about like, this is how the underground man represents, you know, the meaningless of life, or do you think it would be easier to talk about the story, like, more generally?"	0.40 (3)
Prompting, hinting, demonstrating	"So if you were to, you know, if you were to say "Cosmo Girl targets... what?" (prompting) [Used to get the student writer to see that there is more to "punishment." The student elaborated afterwards with "Oh, like, right and wrong."] "So it also demonstrates punishment. Just punishment in general." (hinting) [Used when showing a website exemplifying APA citations.] "Like this. They give you like 'You should have a cover page that does this.' That we don't want you to pay attention to. (demonstrating)	0.24 (3)
Total		10.54 (100)

The following excerpt exemplifies how tutors used cognitive scaffolds, especially pumps, to prod students for their ideas. T4 leads off with instruction, a suggestion ("And so maybe you want to talk about both relationships"), and then moves to pumping questions that set boundaries on a potential response:

T4: And so maybe you want to talk about both relationships. Like the comments between both the king and queen cockroaches [and then also the comments that happen

S4: [Mm-hmm

T4: between the husband and wife. [What's a another possibility here?

S4:   [OK.

T4: Besides the dinner party. Is there another?

Throughout this conference and in the dialogue excerpted above, T4 brainstormed with S4 to develop ideas for her essay, turning to pumps to help S4 generate ideas: "What's another possibility here? Besides the dinner party. Is there another?" Although these pumps opened the conversational floor to S4, they also established clear boundaries for S4's response. T4 pumped S4 for a short response, another specific example (besides the dinner party example). With constraining pumps, T4 facilitated an easy and fast response from S4 in order to continue her data gathering about relationships in one of the two short stories that S4 analyzed for her essay.

While it appeared that open-ended pumps were the ones that had the greatest potential to stump students, the following excerpt shows that student writers, at times, had difficulty formulating responses to constrained pumps as well. It also shows how an experienced tutor can salvage such a situation by moving to another strategy, in this case, a forced-choice strategy:

T7: [Reading draft (whispering) and then speaking aloud to the student] OK. Now here you have a—Do you know what part of speech this is?

S7: What part of speech?

T7: Uh huh. Subject, verb, preposition. Multiple choice.

S7: OK.

T7: Which one do you think?

S7: Uh. That would be a verb?

T7: Well, actually, I meant choice A, subject. Choice B, preposition. So a preposition "from." You begin with that preposition [and

S7:   [Right.

T7: you end with the object of your preposition is"basketball." So a good thing to do [would be to put a comma [there because you put

S7:   [Right.   [OK.

T7: a comma after an introductory four-or-more-word prepositional phrase.

T7 began with a constraining pump question: "Do you know what part of speech this is?" Although the literal answer is either "yes" or "no," the student, like most first-language American English speakers, moved to the intended question: "What part of speech is this?" This highly constrained pump has only one answer. However, S7 did not understand, so T7 adapted by switching to the forced-choice strategy—a strategy of providing alternatives. When S7 guessed incorrectly ("Would that be a verb?"), T7 provided the answer and moved on quickly to his real point: commas after introductory phrases. This excerpt not only points to the difficulties students can have when tutors use pumps to ask test-type questions (questions to which they know the answer already) but also to the importance of contingency, a tutor's ability to adapt to rather than get beyond a student's response.

As the excerpt above shows, cognitive scaffolding strategies exist on a continuum of open to constrained. At their most constraining, they solicit answers easy to identify as correct or not correct, and they often have single correct answers. Other than the requirement for a response, they appear, in spirit at least, similar to instruction. At their most open, cognitive scaffolding strategies lead to a wide range of possible responses. But they can also demand so much effort that students have difficulty responding at all.

Motivational Scaffolding: Close Analysis

In a prior study, we described how writing tutors used motivational scaffolds to encourage students to think about their writing and to continue their efforts after the conference (Mackiewicz and Thompson). We delineated how motivational scaffolds correspond to politeness strategies and thus how they help tutors attend to the affective component of tutoring. Like positive politeness, motivational scaffolds can generate rapport and solidarity. As Table 5 indicates, tutors used the showing concern strategy more frequently than all the other motivational scaffolds, followed at a distance by praising.

Table 5. Frequencies and Percentage of Motivational Scaffolding per 10 Minutes.

Motivational Scaffolding Type	Example	Frequency per 10 Minutes (%)
Showing concern	"Do you see what I mean?" (formulaic) "OK. So what do you feel like at this point?" (nonformulaic)	3.32 (49)
Praising	"That's good." (formulaic) "And I think that your paper does a nice job of, of trying to explain you know, that that independence let you go out and do these other things and perhaps to see the world in a different way." (nonformulaic)	1.53 (23)

Motivational Scaffolding Type	Example	Frequency per 10 Minutes (%)
Reinforcing ownership and control	[Used after the tutor and student have revised a sentence.] "And you are still saying everything you were saying. Everything you wanted to say."	0.76 (11)
Being optimistic or using humor	"But they're politicians. What do you expect?"	0.60 (8)
Showing empathy or sympathy	[Used after reading about the student's school experiences.] "Goodness gracious! What kind of school was this? These people sound terrible."	0.55 (8)
Total		6.76 (99[a])

[a] The percentage total equals 99 rather than 100 because of rounding.

Tutors used both formulaic and nonformulaic demonstrations of concern, but the latter seemed to do even more interactional work than their formulaic counterparts. Because tutors created these nonformulaic strategies on the fly, the strategies were targeted and individualized; thus they even more clearly did the positive politeness work of showing tutors' attentiveness to students and their well-being. For example, T4 checked in on S4's state of mind about two-thirds of the way into the conference to determine whether the student could tolerate another conversational topic:

T4: OK. So what do you feel like at this point? Like, before you leave, I feel like we kind of need to get you a working thesis.

S4: Mm-hmm.

T4's preference clearly was to keep the conference going so that the two of them could develop a viable thesis statement; however, T4 also seemed to recognize the potential for the student to become overwhelmed if she took on yet another task. With her question "So what do you feel like at this point?" T4 gave S4 an opportunity to opt out of continuing, prioritizing the student's well-being and goodwill over her own preferences for the conference agenda. Thus, she used motivational scaffolding to adapt her tutoring to what the student could tolerate at that time. Nonformulaic demonstrations of concern like this one allowed tutors to target their assessments of students' states of mind—potentially gathering more information than a formulaic "you know?" or "see what I mean?" might generate.

Conclusion

Examining scaffolding and instruction helps us better understand the talk that goes on in writing centers. The tutors in this study used a range of tutoring strategies to help students move forward in completing tasks and developing expertise. They most often used the instructional strategies of telling and suggesting, the cognitive scaffolding strategy of pumping, and the motivational scaffolding strategy of showing concern.

Like most research, our study has limitations. First, as previously stated, all of the conferences we analyzed involved tutors and students who spoke American English as a first language. Our participants do not represent the diversity common in and embraced by writing centers. Research about scaffolding infrequently examines its usefulness for learning in cultures other than Western ones (see Williams for an exception). Second, although we speculate about students' responses to tutors in our excerpts, we focus primarily on tutors' talk, forefronting tutors' verbal strategies (see Cazden; Mehan; and Nassaji and Wells for studies with similar goals). These limitations may provide goals for future investigations of scaffolding.

Our findings support those from others concluding that, regardless of the angst sometimes associated with directiveness, tutors often directly (via telling) and indirectly (via suggestions) provide advice. However, unlike early and fairly simplistic predictions of negating learning opportunities or taking control from students, our analysis reveals that these experienced tutors used instruction in complex and sophisticated ways. For example, as we examined above, some tutors provided instruction for students to implement after the conference. Further, tutors sometimes followed instruction with pumping to stimulate students' thinking and to require at least minimal participation in conferences. Also, tutors sometimes ended an instructional sequence with a motivational scaffolding question such as "Do you understand?" Although research shows that students are often unable to gauge their own comprehension (Graesser and Person), such questions provide opportunities for students to at least consider the extent to which they understand and also encourage dialogue. Rather than shutting down students' thinking by providing an answer, these tutors opened up possibilities, providing new directions for students to pursue during and after conferences.

In addition, instruction may be important for developing rapport with students. If, as other writing center studies conclude, students expect tutors to be directive, instruction may be important for building students' trust, maintaining students' attention, and encouraging students' active participation in conferences. Indeed, research has shown that getting their questions answered highly correlates with students' conference satisfaction (Thompson et al.). Finally, Thonus ("Dominance") postulates that tutors who give instruction may in some cases signal solidarity through implying equal status with students. In a study of directive language that examined the variables of gender and first-language American English proficiency, Thonus found that males who spoke American English as a first language received the most advice. She speculates that tutors' willingness to offer advice may have been "an expression of solidarity rather than dominance, if these males [were] considered more powerful (and thus more deserving of assistance)" than females who spoke American English as a first language as well as males and females whose first language was not American English (241). Hence, the use of instructional strategies may indicate that, as institutional representatives, tutors act on what they perceive as a symmetrical (or near symmetrical) relationship with certain students. If this interpretation is correct, early advice about writing center tutoring is not only incorrect but possibly works against rapport building and conference effectiveness.

Along with problematizing instruction and directiveness in writing center conferences, our study demonstrates the complexity of adapting in light of students' responses, an essential aspect of scaffolding. These 10 experienced tutors skillfully adapted their tutoring to students' responses. However, even though our data show tutors moving on, fading, after they instructed students on discrete issues related to style and correctness and occasionally after developing ideas during brainstorming, we did not see the students taking over and controlling the writing tasks. Instead, tutors handed over the tasks because the conference ended. To add further complexity, as shown in the excerpt of T9 and S9, instruction and scaffolding can continue after the conferences end without the tutor being physically present.

Our analysis reveals a great deal about the frequencies with which our tutors used instructional and scaffolding strategies and about combinations of those strategies. However, perhaps its greatest research contribution is the detailed descriptions of instruction, cognitive scaffolding, and motivational scaffolding required to develop the coding scheme. First, the descriptions provide a rigorous, data- and theory-driven framework for future research about instruction and scaffolding in writing centers and for discussions of these strategies in training practicums. Second, the meager research about scaffolding in the teaching of writing uses the brief and unrefined descriptions from Wood, Bruner, and Ross's and Wood and Middleton's articles from the 1970s. We used more recent research that draws on Wood, Bruner, and Ross's germinal study but takes into account the many studies of scaffolding conducted since the 1970s. Our study has been theoretically influenced by research in cognitive psychology, which also influenced Linda Flower and John R. Hayes's view of writing as a process (see Carter for a discussion) and research in linguistics (Brown and Levinson). Since the late 1980s, writing studies has moved almost entirely away from research influenced by cognitive psychology, with its connection to education, and from research in linguistics, with its concern for detailed and replicable descriptions of language in use. We are not arguing that research in cognitive psychology or that linguistic descriptions alone provide adequate ways of discussing writing; however, we do argue that research inspired by cognitive psychology (as well as social psychology) and linguistics can yield important theoretical and methodological insights.

Finally, this study highlights the importance of extensive tutor training in writing centers. Our experienced tutors obviously drew from a range of cognitively taxing and complex strategies as they worked with students. They appeared to have internalized their strategies and were able to draw on them quickly and with flexibility as the tutoring situation warranted and according to the responses from students. Developing this range of strategies requires both knowledge and practice. The descriptions of tutoring strategies we provide can help build this knowledge. By discussing and practicing these strategies in role-playing scenarios, inexperienced tutors may be able to internalize them and draw on them in the confusion of conferences. Further, if writing center directors audio or, preferably, video record and review conferences, they can comment upon tutors' appropriate use of strategies in tutors' evaluations. Hence, writing center directors can instruct and scaffold tutors in how to instruct and scaffold students.

Works Cited

Ashton-Jones, Evelyn. "Asking the Right Questions: A Heuristic for Tutors." *Writing Center Journal* 9.1 (1998): 29–36. Print.

Babcock, Rebecca Day, Kellye Manning, and Travis Rogers. *A Synthesis of Qualitative Studies of Writing Center Tutoring, 1983–2006.* New York: Peter Lang, 2012. Print.

Bandura, Albert. *Self-Efficacy: The Exercise of Control.* New York: Freeman, 1997. Print.

Bell, Diana Calhoun, Holly Arnold, and Rebecca Haddock. "Linguistic Politeness and Peer Tutoring." *Learning Assistance Review* 14.1 (2009): 37–54. Print.

Boyer, Kristy Elizabeth, et al. "Balancing Cognitive and Motivational Scaffolding in Tutorial Dialogue." *Intelligent Tutoring Systems: 9th International Conference on Intelligent Tutoring Systems, ITS 2008, Montreal, Canada, June 23–27, 2008, Proceedings.* Eds. Beverly Woolf, Esma Aimeur, Roger Nkambou, and Susanne Lajoie. Berlin: Springer, 2008. 239–49. Print.

Bransford, John D., Ann L. Brown, and Rodney R. Cocking. *How People Learn: Brain, Mind, Experience, and School.* 2nd ed. Washington, DC: Natl. Acad. P, 2003. Print.

Brooks, Jeff. "Minimalist Tutoring: Making the Student Do All the Work." *Writing Lab Newsletter* 15.6 (1991): 1–4. Print.

Brown, Penelope, and Stephen C. Levinson. *Politeness: Some Universals in Language Usage*. Cambridge: Cambridge UP, 1987. Print.

Bruning, Roger, and Christy Horn. "Developing Motivation to Write." *Educational Psychologist* 35.1 (2000): 25–38. Print.

Bye, Dorothea, Dolores Pushkar, and Michael Conway. "Motivation, Interest, and Positive Affect in Traditional and Nontraditional Undergraduate Students." *Adult Education Quarterly* 57.2 (2007): 141–58. Print.

Carino, Peter, and Doug Enders. "Does Frequency of Visits to the Writing Center Increase Student Satisfaction?" *Writing Center Journal* 22.1 (2001): 83–103. Print.

Carter, Michael. "Problem Solving Reconsidered: A Pluralistic Theory of Problems." *College English* 50.5 (1988): 551–65. Print.

Cazden, Courtney. *Classroom Discourse: The Language of Teaching and Learning*. 2nd ed. Portsmouth: Heinemann, 2001. Print.

Chi, Michelene T. H. "Constructing Self-Explanations and Scaffolded Explanations in Tutoring." *Applied Cognitive Psychology* 10.7 (1996): 33–49. Print.

Chi, Michelene T. H., Miriam Bassok, Matthew W. Lewis, Peter Reimann, and Robert Glaser. "Self-Explanations: How Students Study and Use Examples in Learning to Solve Problems." *Cognitive Science* 13.2 (1989): 145–82. Print.

Chi, Michelene T. H., Nicholas De Leeuw, Mei-Hung Chiu, and Christian LaVancher. "Eliciting Self-Explanations Improves Understanding." *Cognitive Science* 18.3 (1994): 439–77. Print.

Clark, Irene. "Perspectives on the Directive/Non-Directive Continuum in the Writing Center." *Writing Center Journal* 22.1 (2001): 33–58. Print.

Clark, Irene, and Dave Healy. "Are Writing Centers Ethical?" *Writing Program Administration* 20.1/2 (1996): 32–48. Print.

Cromley, Jennifer G., and Roger Azevedo. "What Do Reading Tutors Do? A Naturalistic Study of More and Less Experienced Tutors in Reading." *Discourse Processes* 40.2 (2005): 83–113. Print.

Davis, Kevin M., et al. "The Function of Talk in the Writing Conference: A Study of Tutorial Conversation." *Writing Center Journal* 9.1 (1988): 45–51. Print.

DeCheck, Natalie. "The Power of Common Interest for Motivating Writers: A Case Study." *Writing Center Journal* 32.1 (2012): 28–38. Print.

Evens, Martha, and Joel Michael. *One on One Tutoring by Humans and Computers*. Mahwah: Lawrence Erlbaum, 2006. Print.

Flower, Linda, and John R. Hayes. "A Cognitive Process Theory of Writing." *CCC* 32.4 (1981): 356–87. Print.

Graesser, Arthur C., and Natalie K. Person. "Question Asking During Tutoring." *American Educational Research Journal* 31.1 (1994): 104–37. Print.

Harris, Muriel. "Collaboration Is Not Collaboration Is Not Collaboration: Writing Center Tutorials vs. Peer Response Groups." *CCC* 43.3 (1992): 369–83. Print.

Healy, Dave. "A Defense of Dualism: The Writing Center and the Classroom." *Writing Center Journal* 14 (1993): 16–29. Print.

Hidi, Suzanne, and Pietro Boscolo. "Motivation and Writing." *Handbook of Writing Research*. Eds. Charles A. MacArthur, Steve Graham, and Jill Fitzgerald. New York: Guilford P, 2006. 144–70. Print.

Holton, Derek, and David Clark. "Scaffolding and Metacognition." *International Journal of Mathematical Education in Science and Technology* 37.2 (2006): 127–43. Print.

Kiedaisch, Jean, and Sue Dinitz. "Look Back and Say 'So What': The Limitations of the Generalist Tutor." *Writing Center Journal* 14.1 (1993): 63–75. Print.

Kintsch, Eileen. "Comprehension Theory as a Guide for the Design of Thoughtful Questions." *Topics in Language Disorders* 25.1 (2005): 51–64. Print.

Landis, J. Richard, and Gary G. Koch. "The Measurement of Observer Agreement for Categorical Data." *Biometrics* 33.1 (1977): 159–74. Print.

Lehman, Blair, et al. "What Are You Feeling? Investigating Student Affective States during Expert Human Tutoring Sessions." *Intelligent Tutoring Systems: 9th International Conference on Intelligent Tutoring Systems, ITS 2008, Montreal, Canada, June 23–27, 2008, Proceedings*. Eds. Beverly Woolf, Esma Aimeur, Roger Nkambou, and Susanne Lajoie. Berlin: Springer, 2008. 50–59. Print.

Lepper, Mark R., and Jennifer Henderlong. "Turning 'Play' into 'Work' and 'Work' into 'Play': 25 Years of Research on Intrinsic Motivation Versus Extrinsic Motivation." *Intrinsic and Extrinsic Motivation: The Search for Optional Motivation and Performance*. Eds. Carol Sansone and Judith M. Harackiewicz. San Diego: Acad. P, 2000. 257–307. Print.

Lustick, David. "The Priority of the Question: Focus Questions for Sustained Reasoning in Science." *Journal of Science Teacher Education* 21.5 (2010): 495–511. Print.

Mackiewicz, Jo. "The Effects of Tutor Expertise in Engineering Writing: A Linguistic Analysis of Writing Tutors' Comments." *IEEE Transactions on Professional Communication* 47.4 (2004): 316–28. Print.

—. "Functions of Formulaic and Nonformulaic Compliments on Interactions About Technical Writing." *IEEE Transactions on Professional Communication* 49.1 (2006): 12–25. Print.

Mackiewicz, Jo, and Kathryn Riley. "The Technical Editor as Diplomat: Linguistic Strategies for Balancing Clarity and Politeness." *Technical Communication* 50.1 (2003): 83–94. Print.

Mackiewicz, Jo, and Isabelle Thompson. "Motivational Scaffolding, Politeness, and Writing Center Tutoring." *Writing Center Journal* 33.1 (2013): 38–69. Print.

Mehan, Hugh. *Learning Lessons: Social Organization in the Classroom*. Cambridge: Harvard UP, 1979. Print.

Murphy, Susan Wolff. "'Just Chuck It: I Mean, Don't Get Fixed on It': Self Presentation in Writing Center Discourse." *Writing Center Journal* 26.1 (2006): 62–82. Print.

Nassaji, Hossein, and Gordon Wells. "What's the Use of 'Triadic Dialogue'?: An Investigation of Teacher-Student Interaction." *Applied Linguistics* 21.3 (2000): 376–406. Print.

North, Stephen. "The Idea of a Writing Center." *College English* 46.5 (1984): 433–46. Print.

Pajares, Frank, and Gio Valiante. "Self-Efficacy Beliefs and Motivation in Writing Development." *Handbook of Writing Research*. Eds. Charles A. MacArthur, Steve Graham, and Jill Fitzgerald. New York: Guilford P, 2008. 158–70. Print.

Pemberton, Michael. "Introduction to 'The Function of Talk in the Writing Center Conference: A Study of Tutorial Conversation'." *Writing Center Journal* 30.1 (2010): 23–26. Print.

Person, Natalie. K., et al. "Pragmatics and Pedagogy: Conversational Rules and Politeness Strategies May Inhibit Effective Tutoring." *Cognition and Instruction* 13.2 (1995): 161–88. Print.

Piazza, Roberta. "The Pragmatics of Conducive Questions in Academic Discourse." *Journal of Pragmatics* 34.5 (2002): 509–27. Print.

Puntambekar, Sadhana, and Roland Hübscher. "Tools for Scaffolding Students in a Complex Learning Environment: What Have We Gained and What Have We Missed?" *Educational Psychologist* 40.1 (2005): 1–12. Print.

Putnam, Ralph T. "Structuring and Adjusting Content for Students: A Live and Simulated Tutoring of Addition." *American Educational Research Journal* 24.1 (1987): 13–48. Print.

Rose, C. P., et al. "The Role of Why Questions in Effective Human Tutoring." *Artificial Intelligence in Education* 13 (2003): 55–62. Print.

Severino, Carol. "Rhetorically Analyzing Collaboration(s)." *Writing Center Journal* 13.1 (1992): 53–64. Print.

Shamoon, Linda K., and Deborah H. Burns. "A Critique of Pure Tutoring." *Writing Center Journal* 15.2. (1995): 134–52. Print.

Shell, Duane F., Carolyn Colvin Murphy, and Roger H. Bruning. "Self-Efficacy and Outcome Expectancy Mechanisms in Reading and Writing Achievement." *Journal of Educational Psychology* 81.1 (1989): 91–100. Print.

Smith, Heather, and Steve Higgins. "Opening Classroom Interaction: The Importance of Feedback." *Cambridge Journal of Education* 36.4 (2006): 485–502. Print.

Stone, C. Addison. "The Metaphor of Scaffolding: Its Utility for the Field of Learning Disabilities." *Journal of Learning Disabilities* 31.4 (1998): 344–64. Print.

Tharp, Roland, and Ronald Gallimore. *Rousing Minds to Life: Teaching, Learning, and Schooling in Social Context*. Cambridge: Cambridge UP, 1988. Print.

Thompson, Isabelle. "Scaffolding in the Writing Center: A Microanalysis of an Experienced Tutor's Verbal and Nonverbal Tutoring Strategies." *Written Communication* 26.4 (2009): 417–53. Print.

Thompson, Isabelle, and Jo Mackiewicz. "Questions in Writing Center Conferences." *Writing Center Journal* 33.2 (2014): 37–70. Print.

Thompson, Isabelle, et al. "Examining Our Lore: A Survey of Students' and Tutors' Satisfaction with Writing Center Conferences." *The Writing Center Journal* 29.1 (2009): 78–106. Print.

Thonus, Terese. "Dominance in Academic Writing Tutorials: Gender, Language Proficiency, and the Offering of Suggestions." *Discourse & Society* 10.2 (1999): 225–48. Print.

—. "How To Communicate Politely and Be a Tutor, Too: NS–NNS Interaction and Writing Center Practice." *Text* 19.2 (1999): 253–79. Print.

—. "Triangulation in the Writing Center: Tutor, Tutee, and Instructor Perceptions of the Tutor's Role." *Writing Center Journal* 21.3 (2001): 59–82. Print.

—. "Tutor and Student Assessments of Academic Writing Tutorials: What Is 'Success'?" *Assessing Writing* 8.2 (2002): 110–34. Print.

Thornbury, Scott, and Diana Slade. *Conversation: From Description to Pedagogy.* Cambridge: Cambridge UP, 2006. Print.

Tienken, Christopher, Stephanie Goldberg, and Dominic DiRocco. "Questioning the Questions." *Education Digest* 46.1 (2010): 28–32. Web. 27 Sept. 2011.

Trimbur, John. "Peer Tutoring: A Contradiction in Terms." *Writing Center Journal* 7.2 (1987): 21–28. Print.

Vygotsky, Lev Semenovich. *Mind and Society: The Development of Higher Psychological Processes*. Cambridge: Harvard UP, 1978. Print.

Williams, Jessica. "Tutoring and Revision: Second Language Writers in the Writing Center." *Journal of Second Language Writing* 13.3 (2004): 173–201. Print.

Wolcott, Willa. "Talking It Over: A Qualitative Study of Writing Center Conferencing." *Writing Center Journal* 9.2 (1989): 15–29. Print.

Wood, David, Jerome S. Bruner, and Gail Ross. "The Role of Tutoring in Problem Solving." *Journal of Child Psychology and Psychiatry* 17.2 (1976): 89–100. Print.

Wood, David, and David Middleton. "A Study of Assisted Problem-Solving." *British Journal of Psychology* 66.2 (1975): 181–91. Print.

Zimmerman, Barry. J. "Academic Studying and the Development of Personal Skill: A Self-Regulatory Perspective." *Educational Psychologist* 3.2/3 (1998): 73–86. Print.

Zimmerman, Barry. J., and Anastasia Kitsantas. "Acquiring Writing Revision Skill: Shifting from Process to Outcome Self-regulatory Goals." *Journal of Educational Psychology* 91.2 (1999): 1–10. Print.

Zimmerman, Barry. J., and Dale H. Schunk. *Self-Regulated Learning and Academic Achievement: Theoretical Perspectives*. 2nd ed. Mahwah, NJ: Erlbaum, 2001. Print.

Course Design

Seoul Searching: Transitioning Basic Writers Within the Global Frontiers Project

Tabetha Adkins and Connie Meyer
Texas A&M University–Commerce

The course we describe here was designed especially for students enrolled in a collaborative program between Texas A&M University–Commerce and Konkuk University in South Korea. This course was created specifically for students who did not earn a qualifying score on a standardized placement exam required of all first-year students for enrollment into "college-level" English 1301. For this course, a team consisting of several graduate teaching assistants, instructors, a linguistic specialist, and the writing program administrator combined strategies for teaching basic writing and English as a second language (ESL) to create a pilot "sheltered instruction" program, one that provided additional support to all Korean students enrolled in basic writing courses. This support included an additional "lab" that each student was required to attend; their lab teacher was present in each English 1301 class, as well, to answer questions and support instruction. Every Konkuk student enrolled in the pilot program passed the course and enrolled in English 1302 along with their cohorts who were considered "college ready."

Institutional Context

In the fall of 2012, our university commenced a program in collaboration with Konkuk University in Seoul and Chungjua, South Korea. According to the university's English language website, Konkuk University is a private metropolitan research university with approximately 26,000 students. Conversely, Texas A&M University–Commerce is a public rural university in Commerce, Texas with approximately 12,000 students. According to the agreement between the two universities, students who enroll in the collaborative program titled The Global Frontiers Program complete one semester of intensive English language instruction at Konkuk University before coming to northeast Texas to earn Texas A&M University–Commerce bachelor's degrees. During the first semester, 149 Konkuk students qualified and participated in the program. Students enrolled in this program major in everything from Spanish to physics and live on campus in a university dorm.

Once these students complete their intensive English language instruction, they are fully accepted into the university and therefore complete the same steps required of all other students. In Texas, this means that students are required to take a placement exam that determines whether or not they are prepared for college-level reading, writing, and math. Students are required to attain a designated score, and those who do not take "basic" or "remedial" courses designed to, as administrators often say, make these students college ready. Of the 149 students enrolled in the Global Frontiers Program, 100 or 67% placed into the "basic" course and were involved with the program we describe here.

To explain the context of this course, we must preface this information with some history about our writing program. In previous years, students who were designated as not college ready were required to take English 100, a three-hour class that included a smaller, two-hour lab where students received more personalized attention and help with their writing assignments. Though the course carried no credit toward graduation, students were required to complete English 100 before moving on to English 1301.

The course was not efficient under this old model. We have come to understand basic writing and basic writing courses much like David Bartholomae, who famously writes that "basic writing programs have become expressions of our desire to produce basic writers, to maintain the course, the argument, and the slot in the university community; to maintain the distinction (basic/normal) we have learned to think through and by" (174). At our institution, basic writing did not fully serve our so-called basic writers. Failure rates were high and most students had to retake the course, only to follow the course up with English 1301, which resembled English 100 a great deal. Because Texas dictates through the Texas Success Initiative that students with low college entrance exam scores take a basic writing or remedial course, we could not simply eliminate the course and mainstream students as many universities choose to do. Instead, we adopted a "mainstream with support" model. English 100 was converted into a three-hour lab designed to support English 1301 for students with low entrance exam scores. Once students pass the course, they move on to English 1302 with their cohorts whose test scores did not require a remedial or basic course. We believe that this model has removed redundancy from an otherwise cohesive first-year curriculum, and the pass rate improved by an incredible 44%. When we learned that the Konkuk students would be coming to our program and individual students would have differing levels of English training, we decided to take advantage of the existing courses while creating programming that would help students both improve their English speaking and master the concepts of English 1301.

In the next section, we detail the theoretical rationale informing the four major concepts at work in this curriculum: writing about writing, basic writing instruction, sheltered instruction, and the cultural considerations we made for our Korean students.

Theoretical Rationales

Writing About Writing

Since 2011, our writing program has operated under the writing about writing approach. This approach, first introduced by Doug Downs and Elizabeth Wardle in a 2007 *CCC* article, "explores reading and writing: How does writing work? How do people use writing? What are problems related to writing and reading and how can they be solved?" (558). We liked this approach for several reasons. First, we wanted our students to learn about our discipline. We admired the model commonly seen in sciences, social sciences, and other subjects where students learn the basic methods, concepts, and theories that create a discipline. We see writing studies as a discipline that has its own methodologies, concepts, and theories, so we did not want to create a program where we had to "invent" content. Some examples of invented content might be assignments where students can research anything, or courses built around themes like paranormal activity, films, presidential campaigns, et cetera. We agree with Downs and Wardle's argument that "when the course content is writing studies, writing instructors are concretely enabled to fill that expert-reader role" (559). If the invented content permits students to study anything, instructor expertise is more difficult to ensure. In our view, this expertise is important because, as Downs and Wardle argue, it is our responsibility as writing professionals to correct misconceptions about writing that are prevalent in society.

Under this writing about writing framework, our two-course first-year writing sequence helps students learn about writing, research, and reading. In the first course, using Downs and Wardle's textbook *Writing About Writing*, students study concepts like the Burkean Parlor, John Swales' CARS (Creating a Research Space) model and discourse community concept, writing processes, and the relationship between reader and writer. In the second course, students build on the framework they developed in the first course and treat literacy, discourse communities, or literacy artifacts in context by completing small-scale literacy ethnographies (4). In these literacy ethnographies, students are required not only to report on their observation data but also to contextualize that data within the frame of other scholarship. We believe this course aligns with what Downs and Wardle had in mind when they wrote, "through primary research, students begin to learn that careful observation and empirical data-gathering techniques bolster their authority and reduce their reliance on other experts' pronouncements" (563).

We piloted the writing about writing approach one semester before the Korean students arrived. We soon realized that this approach is challenging because it asks students to interact with texts typically written for academics, but we also liked this curriculum *because* of the challenges it posed. In our program, we believe that students should be challenged with difficult content. We knew that this challenge might be especially difficult for our Korean students who were experiencing a new culture, curriculum, and teaching and learning style all in a language that is not their first. Because we wanted the Global Frontiers Program to be successful, we knew we would have to provide different forms of curricular support to our new students. We supplemented the curriculum in two ways: through the use of rhetorical dexterity and sheltered instruction, both of which are described below.

Rhetorical Dexterity

In her 2008 book *The Way Literacy Lives: Rhetorical Dexterity and Basic Writing Instruction*, Shannon Carter describes "a pedagogy of rhetorical dexterity" as "a pedagogical approach that develops in students the ability to read, understand, manipulate, and negotiate the cultural and linguistic codes of a new community of practice based on a relatively accurate assessment of another, more familiar one" (14). In this case, the "more familiar one" was the academic conventions these students of the highly selective, private Konkuk University had likely mastered in their home language. Instructors often encouraged our Korean students to write about the differences and similarities between the reading and writing they had done in their home country and the reading and writing they were studying in our program. We found this strategy to be a useful way to help students navigate the complex concepts inherent in the writing about writing approach. Students often talked about writing in high school, but also referenced, as Carter suggests, "vernacular literacies—video game literacies, Star Trek literacies, and comic book literacies, among other things" (13). An additional benefit of this approach was a cultural one: Korean students learned more about the American culture and academics for which they had traveled so far, and American students (and instructors) learned about Korean culture, education, popular culture, and people.

Sheltered Instruction

The final theoretical frame for this course is a pedagogical approach called sheltering. This model is most commonly utilized at the K–12 levels. According to David Freeman and Yvonne Freeman, this model, often abbreviated as SDAIE (Specifically Designed Academic Instruction in English), was developed specifically to help limited English-proficient (LEP) students "develop their cognitive academic language proficiency (CALP)—the kind of proficiency required to make sense of academic language in context-reduced situations" (2). Freeman and Freeman list the following as typical sheltering activities:

> Extralinguistic cues such as visuals, props, and body language; linguistic modifiers such as repetition and pauses during speech; interactive lectures with frequent comprehension checks; cooperative learning strategies; focus on central concepts rather than on details by using a thematic approach; development of reading strategies such as mapping and writing to develop thinking. (2)

Obviously, the fields of linguistics and language learning have made great strides in the twenty to thirty years that have elapsed since sheltered instruction was first employed to help non-native speakers of English, but this system is still used with good effect today in school systems with high numbers of non-native or non-proficient speakers of English, including the Dallas Independent School System here in northeast Texas.

In addition to the success this program has enjoyed, there are several incentives to employ a program like the one we describe here. As linguist David Crystal shows, of the two billion English users in the world, 1.6 billion are non-native speakers, which means there are far more non-native speakers of English in the world than native speakers. This population creates an enormous opportunity for English educators. And recent surveys by The Institute of International Education indicate that more and more, these non-native speakers are choosing to study in the United States. In their November 2012 "Open Doors Report on International Education Exchange," the institute reported a 6.5% increase in international students studying in the United States from the 2010–2011 academic year—this adds up to 764,495 international students in the United States for the 2011–2012 academic year. Students included in these numbers originate from many different countries, but the highest numbers of students come first from China, then India, and finally South Korea, who sent 72,295 students to study in the United States during the 2011–2012 academic year. Of the over 700,000 international students studying in the United States, 28%, or 219,853, are undergraduates who may have the opportunity to participate in and benefit from programs like the one we describe here. Of course, in recent composition scholarship, there have been several academic movements aimed at addressing this growing population, including multilingualism (Horner, NeCamp, and Donahue; Lu and Horner), translingualism (Horner, et. al), World Englishes and English as a lingua franca (Canagarajah), multiliteracies (The New London Group), and responses from organizations like the CCCC.

A second incentive for adoption of this model is a financial one—though we want to acknowledge our discomfort with the concept of recruiting students for financial gain. Universities are often motivated by business models or formula funding, and thus we cannot ignore the tremendous financial benefit of increased international student populations for campuses like Texas A&M University–Commerce. The 149 South Korean students involved in the Global Frontiers Program in the Spring 2012 semester, as residents of South Korea, paid out-of-state tuition here in Texas. This program led to an additional three million dollars in tuition revenue for the university in that semester alone. Obviously, in times of budget cuts and financial uncertainty, there is an immense (if troubling) impetus for this program to be successful and to lead to additional student participation. This situation, paired with the fact that the writing program was the only program on campus that made special preparations for our Global Frontiers students, put the writing program in a unique leadership position on campus.

Finally, another benefit of this course design is that it keeps actual remedial course hours at a minimum. In our model, students only take three hours of remedial courses—the lab—while they are concurrently enrolled in three hours of "college-level" first-year writing. Administrators at Texas A&M University–Commerce like this model because students do not have to "sit out" a semester in remedial course work before moving on to their college-level courses. In a time when funds for so-called developmental education are disappearing, this model may be a viable option for others as well. For example, in the state of Texas, developmental education courses are supposed to be phased out or outsourced to community colleges, according to the coordinating board's current plan, by the year 2020. Creating a non-course laboratory or even tutoring that follows this model may be one way to continue providing support to basic writers or English newcomers like the students enrolled in the Global Frontiers program while they complete their college-level course work.

Critical Reflection

As we discussed earlier, we employed Carter's model of rhetorical dexterity, sheltering, ESL/EFL instruction, and writing about writing to address this unique student demographic, thus constructing a new model for basic writing instruction. This model trains writers to effectively read, understand, manipulate, and negotiate the cultural and linguistic codes of a new community of practice based on a relatively accurate assessment of another, more recognizable one, which then allows basic writers the rhetorical dexterity to adapt to literacy expectations of the new community. As the student body at universities in the United States becomes more diverse, this methodology provides a template for working with any ESL group. In addition, we found that we had to address unexpected cultural variations in beliefs about writing. Upon completion of our project we were able to form conclusions concerning the curriculum and support found within our program as well as access unexpected outcomes.

Curriculum

Writing about writing is a flexible pedagogy that allows students to reflect on their own writing methodology without the distraction of external components that would detract them from internalizing and exploring their individual writing styles and goals. Konkuk students were more comfortable working with empirical evidence and external sources, resisting assignments that required a reflective or autobiographical component. We suspect this resistance was culturally reinforced as they claimed they were unfamiliar with projects that were introspective or exploratory. Thus the flexible pedagogy allowed Konkuk students to more clearly analyze their own choices about writing and organization by focusing their writing on an intrinsically familiar forum—their own writing processes.

In keeping with the philosophy of a flexible pedagogy, we felt offering students various essay models from the text for each unit allowed them the security of a format, without encouraging conformity to any one model. This reflects Carter's theories about a form of rhetorical dexterity that exposes students to the expectations of the "new" community as they transition from their former community. We found, however, that we had to provide extra support for textbook essays that contained specialized jargon less accessible to ESL students and content focused on cultural references and analogies with which they were not familiar. To address these issues, in-class exercises allowed us to introduce Americanized ideas and concepts in context. Groups analyzed American versus Korean flash mob content, for instance, which encouraged students to compare performance art through the lens of both cultures. Predictably, Korean students, like most students, were most comfortable writing about concepts and ideas centered on their native culture. We also encouraged students to access self-reflective, complex issues involving identity, class, and gender in the writing about writing approach by viewing these topics through their own interests in fashion, sports, films, video games, or so-called online "affinity spaces" (Gee).

Support Components

This program required concentrated coordination between classroom and lab instructors, writing center tutors, the director of first-year writing, and the department linguistic specialist. Weekly meetings between Meyer (the Konkuk Coordinator) and instructors addressed classroom strategies, both successful and failed, and synchronized assignments and expectations. These meetings provided us opportunities to gather various data about the Konkuk students' capabilities and strengths as well as their limitations, both as ESL students and as basic writers. Data from these meetings were subsequently relayed to the director and linguistic specialist for additional transparency and recording purposes.

Student conferences were also a critical component of our pedagogical practice as students were reluctant to seek clarity or support in class. The collective nature of their culture, compounded by students' limited English skills, fostered their in-class reticence. However, individual conferences allowed students to express concerns and seek assistance. These conferences also allowed instructors to measure linguistic comprehension on a personalized level and thus construct perimeters while adjusting expectations. Expanded English comprehension meant that more nuanced and complex concepts could be introduced into the classroom and revised benchmarks could be established. Individuals needing extra clarification and support could be identified. Stronger students, who began to serve as interpreters, were also revealed through these conferences.

Konkuk students, unlike many basic writers, were accustomed to receiving high grades at their own university, and as a result, these students were willing to work very hard through multiple revisions to improve their grades. They also became anxious if they did not receive very precise rubrics and writing prompts. They took advantage of office hours and conferences to secure their understanding of what was expected of them for upcoming assignments and to clarify instructors' expectations. Many basic writers, often unfamiliar with support systems available in a university system, have minimal involvement with instructors or tutors outside of the classroom. Conversely, our Konkuk students wanted full access to our university support systems. We found they appreciated the opportunity for multiple revisions, brainstorming sessions, and student conferences. They also appreciated detailed, focused revision instruction, and very explicit, weighted rubrics.

There were three main components utilized to assist students' progress: visual aids, two-hour labs, and writing center assistance. For ESL basic writers, we found that all course content must be visually accessible and permanently available in order to provide the highest level of impact. Class lectures, writing heuristics, essay rubrics, and writing guides were posted on the classroom website. All materials, including lecture notes, were displayed on the classroom video screen during class lectures. As part of the sheltering component of our project, Korean terms were often displayed alongside their English translations for a more comprehensive understanding of course material. We heeded the advice of scholars like Yu Ren Dong who calls on teachers of non-native speakers to "diversify teaching strategies when dealing with diverse students" (378). She also illustrates another point we carefully considered:

> [C]omposition instructors need information about students' native literacy learning in order to tailor their instruction. In getting to know students and their home literacy backgrounds, teachers send the message that ESL students' home literacy backgrounds are acknowledged and valued rather than dismissed or ignored. (378)

In addition, getting to know students on a personal level through conferences, in-class discussion, and their writing helped instructors implement the strategies based on Carter's theory of rhetorical dexterity. Learning about students' interests and hobbies helped us develop examples that would interest the students and illustrate complex concepts.

Konkuk students also benefited substantially from basic grammar instruction. Although most basic writers need or want grammatical training, we did not expect the need to implement such explicit instruction with this group as they had transferred from a high-performing university and had passed their TESOF exams. We responded by incorporating this component into lab sessions through lectures, writing exercises, and PowerPoint presentations. The students relied heavily on their lab sessions for continuous revision, often focused on grammar. As these lab sessions were smaller, students could receive more personalized and concentrated assistance. This face-to-face writing instruction was a critical component of our approach, and, although the practice is often discounted today, we feel it was critical to our success.

Overall, instructors, including lab instructors and writing center tutors, became familiar with these students' Korean academic expectations, their writing and research training and traditions, and their cultural views about learning and education. These dedicated instructors for the Konkuk project were also aware of the students' particular ESL-related struggles, the expectations of their classroom instructors, and the specifics of the course content. Students seemed to respond to and appreciate the instructors' efforts by utilizing all the resources available to them; the students regularly met with instructors during office hours, created study groups, and made good use of the Writing Center. This extra effort and commitment from instructors and students alike was a critical contributor to the success of the project.

Students depended significantly on the writing center for revision instruction. We found we could communicate much of our expectations through the writing center director, who conveyed those expectations to her staff. All of the writing center tutors had experience tutoring non-native speakers and many had read Muriel Harris and Tony Silvas's article, "Tutoring ESL Students: Issues and

Options," as well as other articles about strategies for teaching English to nonnative speakers. One-on-one attention to a student's unique issues by trained staff, familiar with the course content, provided a third level of reinforcement as well as practice with their verbal skills. These tutoring sessions became much more productive as the semester progressed. The Konkuk students generally provided well-developed first drafts and fully participated in the process of peer review. As a result, they were noticeably more detail-oriented and frank in their comments to their peers in lab sessions. Students also benefited from the extra grammatical and organizational practices included in the process.

Response

In our ongoing assessment of and reflection on this program, we noticed that as students became more familiar with the English language, along with the cultural and academic mores of their adopted academic home, their writing skills strengthened at differing rates and levels. This led to a widening gap in the student work produced in this course. This is a common trend among many basic writers as they begin to engage with ever-more-complicated writing concepts. Nevertheless, this trend frustrated attempts to collectively teach the Konkuk students. At this point, they began to resemble more mainstream writers with more defined levels of competence and strength. We then challenged advanced writers to write more complex final essays with longer lengths, more consulted sources, and more elaborate arguments. Some of these advanced students began to tutor their peers outside of class, a development we rarely see in mainstream basic writing courses.

We also kept individual student status check sheets that were revised weekly. One instructor, Allyson Jones, developed a system by which we could cross-reference students across coursework, lab work, and attendance, allowing us to see trends, both incidental in nature—such as increased absences in their labs or classrooms or missed work—and systemic—such as declining grade point averages due to an inability to comprehend instruction. The results of these reports were sent to the linguistic specialist who coordinated with a representative from the International Affairs Office.

Evaluation

Ultimately, the final course evaluation grades posed an unusual situation and dilemma. Halfway through the term, instructors felt that the students would not be proficient enough to advance to English 1302. We devised alternative strategies to increase student mastery. One constant challenge was the Konkuk students' insularity. They largely did not interact with English speakers as suggested, and as a result their English verbal skills did not improve as quickly as their writing skills. Instructors had to determine how their students' progress should be evaluated holistically, incorporating their progress with English language comprehension, writing organizational skills, and reading comprehension and application. These latter components are considered general standards for evaluating basic writers' progress in most programs, but the ESL component required us to rethink our standards. Instructors decided that they must evaluate students' progress based on these components as they appeared in the students' final drafts, using their final product as a guide.

One particularly challenging component of our course was the students' final project, a "Showcase Piece" designed to allow them to demonstrate an application of their understanding of writing about writing in a unique manner. According to the syllabus, this assignment instructs students to

> create a showcase piece to highlight what you've learned about "Writing About Writing." The medium you select is your choice – you could do a video, a song, a poem, a short story, or a painting... about what writing means to you. You might consider how to represent your initial views of writing and your current views...You should include a typed reflection essay, 4–6 pages discussing the significance of your showcase piece. Analyze what this piece represents to you about writing, and connect your showcase to the issues we've discussed in the course.

Thus, the project required creative, critical thinking from our students as well as a creative application of their writing assignments—often reconstructed in a different medium. Student response was strong and demonstrated scholastic and linguistic agility at levels we had not anticipated. The assignment also required a narration of these projects, requiring students to demonstrate verbal skills at an advanced level. During their presentations, students concluded their lectures with a command of the English language comparable to native speaking students. Their presentations reflected their writing process evolution in creative genres, such as elaborate video clips, PowerPoint presentations, and original musical performances. We felt that this complex task validated our efforts as it provided such tangible evidence that students were able to not only organize their thoughts in a productive manner but also convey them clearly.

Final Reflection

This modified basic writing sheltering program proved successful for 100% of the students enrolled during the pilot semester, and they went on to enroll in 1302 and perform well. The program was also a success for the university since it effectively incorporated a large group of high achieving but contextually at-risk students. Finally, for the first-year writing program at Texas A&M University–Commerce, this program provided a flexible template to be used for future projects, particularly as the university explores options concerning international university exchanges.

Acknowledgement

We want to thank the instructional team for their intellectual input in this program and acknowledge them here by name. Our linguistic specialist was Dr. Lucy Pickering, the fantastic instructors involved in this program were Geoff Clegg, Allyson Jones, John Lewis, John Pierce, and one of the coauthors, Dr. Connie Meyer. Dr. Tabetha Adkins, a coauthor, served as the writing program administrator. We also want to acknowledge the foresight of Dr. Pickering and our Dean, Dr. Salvatore Attardo, to prepare for our South Korean students in a way that made this program a success. Every writing program should be so lucky as to have a linguist in the dean's office.

Works Cited

Bartholomae, David. "The Tidy House: Basic Writing in the American Curriculum." *Journal of Basic Writing* 12.1 (1993): 4-21. Rpt. in *Landmark Essays on Basic Writing*. Ed. Kay Halasek and Nels P. Highberg. Mahway, NJ: Hermagoras P, 2001. 171-184. Print.

Brandt, Deborah. *Literacy in American Lives*. New York: Cambridge UP, 2001. Print.

Canagarajah, A. Suresh. *A Geopolitics of Academic Writing*. Pittsburgh: U of Pittsburgh P, 2002. Print.

Carter, Shannon. *The Way Literacy Lives: Rhetorical Dexterity and Basic Writing Instruction*. Albany, NY: SUNY P, 2008. Print.

"CCCC Statement on Second Language Writing and Writers." *CCCC*. NCTE, Nov. 2009. Web. 26 Oct. 2010.

Crystal, David. "English: A Status Report." *Spotlight* Sept. 2011: 28-33. Web. 22 Mar. 2013.

Dong, Yu Ren. "The Need to Understand ESL Students' Native Language Writing Experiences." *Teaching English in the Two-Year College* 26.3 (1999): 277-85. Print.

Downs, Douglas, and Elizabeth Wardle. "Teaching about Writing, Righting Misconceptions: (Re)visioning 'First-Year Composition' as 'Introduction to Writing Studies.'" *CCC* 58.4 (2007): 552-84. Print.

—. *Writing About Writing: A College Reader*. Boston: Bedford St. Martin's, 2011. Print.

Freeman, David, and Yvonne Freeman. *Sheltered English Instruction*. ERIC Digest. ERIC Publications, 1 Oct. 1988. Web. 31 July 2012.

Gabriel, Trip. "Plagiarism Lines Blur for Students in Digital Age." *New York Times*. New York Times, 1 Aug. 2010. Web. 26 Sept. 2013.

Gee, James Paul. *Situated Language and Learning: A Critique of Traditional Schooling*. London: Routledge, 2004. Print.

Harris, Muriel, and Tony Silva. "Tutoring ESL Students: Issues and Options." *CCC* 44.4 (1993): 525-37. Print.

Horner, Bruce, Min-Zhan Lu, and Paul Kei Matsuda, eds. *Cross-Language Relations in Composition*. Carbondale: SIUP, 2010. Print.

Horner, Bruce, Samantha Necamp, and Christiane Donahue. "Toward a Multilingual Composition Scholarship: From English Only to a Translingual Norm." *CCC* 63.2 (2011): 269-300. Print.

Open Doors Report on International Education Exchange. Institute of International Education, 2013. 25 Oct. 2013. Web. 22 Mar. 2013.

"Sheltered English Instruction." Teaching Diverse Learners. *Educ. Alliance at Brown U*, n.d. Web. 31 July 2012.

Surowiecki, James. *The Wisdom of Crowds*. New York: Anchor P, 2005. Print.

The New London Group. "A Pedagogy of Multiliteracies: Designing Social Futures." *Harvard Educational Review* 66.1 (1996): 60-92. Print.

Wilbur, Richard. "The Writer." *Poets.org*. Acad. of Amer. Poets, Aug. 2003. Web. 26 Sept. 2013.

Syllabus

ENG 1301: College Reading and Writing

Course Description

This course introduces students to writing as an extended, complex, and recursive process and prepares students for English 1302, which more rigorously examines the forms and structures of argument and means to approaching multiple audiences. In 1301 students will write weekly and will work on essay organization and development. The course will emphasize close reading, summarizing, and analysis of expository texts, including student writing.

Course Texts:

Writing About Writing: A College Reader. Elizabeth Wardle and Doug Downs. Bedford St. Martins, 2011. ISBN# 978-0-312-53493-6

Writing at Texas A&M University–Commerce. Tabetha Adkins. Fountainhead, 2011. ISBN #978-59871-474-6

Assessment Criteria Grading Breakdown

Assignments	100% total
How Do I Write?	15%
How Do You Define a Good Academic Argument?	15%
Self-Portrait of a Reader and Writer	15%

Assignments	100% total
Letter to a Literacy Sponsor	15%
Final Project/ Showcase Piece	30%
Participation	10%

Calendar

Key:

Writing About Writing: A College Reader = WAW
Writing at Texas A&M University–Commerce = Guide

Week	Reading Due	Writing Due
1	Adkins, "Plagiarism" (*Guide*) Garbriel, "Plagiarism Lines Blur in Digital Age" article (*The New York Times*)	
2	Swales, "'Create a Research Space': (CARS) Model of Research Introductions" (*WAW*) Greene, "Argument as Conversation: The Role of Inquiry in Writing a Researched Argument" (*WAW*) Kleine, "What Is It We Do When We Write Articles Like This One—And How Do We Get Students To Join Us?" (*WAW*)	
3	Porter, "Intertextuality and the Discourse Community" (*WAW*) Swales, "The Concept of Discourse Community" (*WAW*) Kantz, "Helping Students Use Textual Sources Persuasively" (*WAW*)	Draft of How Do I Write? essay
4	Williams, "The Phenomenology of Error" (*WAW*) Murray, "All Writing is Autobiography" (*WAW*)	How Do I Write? Essay due
5	Goodman, "Calming the Inner Critic and Getting to Work" (*WAW*) King, "What Writing Is" (*WAW*)	

Week	Reading Due	Writing Due
6	Hyland, "Disciplinary Discourses: Social Interactions in Academic Writing" (*WAW*) Revision v. Editing chapter (*Guide*)	Draft of How Do You Define a Good Academic Argument? essay
7	Lamott, "Shitty First Drafts" (*WAW*) Wilbur, "The Writer" Perl, "The Composing Processes of Unskilled College Writers" (*WAW*)	How Do You Define a Good Academic Argument? essay due
8	Berkenkotter, "Decisions and Revisions: The Planning Strategies of a Published Writer" and Murray's response (*WAW*) Tomlinson, "Tuning, Tying, and Training Texts: Metaphors for Revision" (*WAW*) Sontag, "Directions: Write, Read, Rewrite. Repeat Steps 2 and 3 as Needed" (*WAW*) Díaz, "Becoming a Writer" (*WAW*)	
9	Watch *The Social Network* in class	
10	Tierney & Pearson, "Toward a Composing Model of Reading" (*WAW*) Malcolm X, "Learning to Read" (*WAW*)	Draft of Self-Portrait of a Reader and Writer essay
11	Alexie, "The Joy of Reading and Writing: Superman and Me" (*WAW*) Textual analysis chapter (*Guide*) Devoss, et.al. "The Future of Literacy" (*WAW*) Brandt, "Sponsors of Literacy" (*WAW*)	Self-Portrait of a Reader and Writer essay due
12	Wardle, "Identity, Authority, and Learning to Write in New Workplaces" (*WAW*) Mirabelli, "Learning to Serve: The Language and Literacy of Food Service Workers" (*WAW*)	Draft of Letter to a Literacy Sponsor
13	Branick, "Coaches Can Read, Too: An Ethnographic Study of a Football Coaching Discourse Community" (*WAW*)	Letter to a Literacy Sponsor Due
14	Showcase Piece Presentations	
15	Showcase Piece Presentations	

Instruction and Evaluation Criteria For Writing Assignments

1. How Do I Write?

Instructions

Using the model essay found in *Writing About Writing* (pages 292–97), analyze your own writing process or processes. To complete this analysis, you will need to employ one of the strategies or techniques described by the scholars you read in unit one. For example, the sample essay uses Swales' CARS model. In this essay, be explicit about the methodology or analysis tool you're using, and use a lot of examples. The more thorough your analysis, the stronger your essay will be.

Evaluation Criteria
- Essay is clearly modeled after one of the model essays found in *Writing About Writing* (pages 292–97).
- Draft clearly demonstrates a specific writing process.
- The writing process is described in detail.
- Experience is presented effectively, using appropriate narrative techniques.
- Experience is reflected on, not merely presented/related.
- Material is organized logically.
- Sentences are clear, complete, and relatively error free.

2. How Do You Define Good Academic Argument?

Instructions

Now that you've read about academic writing in unit one and different ideas about what makes writing "good" in unit two, it's time to synthesize those two concepts to create your theory of how you personally define a good academic argument. Your theory will be informed by all the texts you have read so far. You might, for example, use these texts to help explain your theory, quote sections of texts that help illustrate your theory, or even point to elements of the texts with which you disagree.

Evaluation Criteria
- Draft clearly describes a specific writing process that demonstrates a personal theory of effective argument.
- Essay includes elements from the model essays found in *Writing About Writing*.
- Experience is presented effectively, using appropriate narrative techniques.
- Material is organized logically.

- Sentences are clear, complete, and relatively error free.

3. Self-Portrait of a Reader and Writer

Instructions

The prompt titled "Assignment Option 2. Portrait of a Writer" on page 325 in *Writing About Writing* asks you to "consider the story you have to tell about yourself as a writer." For this assignment, you will expand that description and "consider the story you have to tell about yourself as a writer" *and* as a reader. How are these two identities if at all, connected for you? What are some positive experiences you have had with reading and writing? When, what, and where do you like to read and write? Use the questions in the prompt (pages 325–27) to help you get started, but be sure to connect your own experiences to the readings from unit three—you'll want to quote from those texts to show the connections between your experiences and the authors' experiences and/or claims.

Evaluation Criteria
- Draft is clearly connected to the readings in unit three found in *Writing About Writing* (Berkenkotter, Sontag, and/or Malcolm X).
- Essay includes a personal narrative describing author's experience as a writer and as a reader.
- Essay includes specific examples of positive experiences related to writing.
- Essay is presented effectively, using appropriate narrative techniques.
- Material is organized logically.
- Sentences are clear, complete, and relatively error free.

4. Letter to a Literacy Sponsor

Instructions

Using Brandt's definition of a literacy sponsor, identify someone who has been a literacy sponsor to you. Using the model essay on pages 271–77 in *Writing About Writing*, compose a letter to the literacy sponsor you've identified, using at least five texts you've read in this course (six counting Brandt) to discuss how their sponsorship has affected you as a reader and/or writer. One objective of this letter is certainly to illustrate that you understand the concept of the literacy sponsor, but another objective is to demonstrate that you can synthesize all the concepts and texts from the course.

Evaluation Criteria
- Draft is clearly connected to the readings in unit three found in *Writing About Writing* regarding literacy sponsors.

- Essay includes a personal narrative describing writer's experience with literary sponsor.
- Essay includes specific examples demonstrating impact of literacy sponsor.
- Essay is presented effectively, using appropriate narrative techniques.
- Material is organized logically.
- Sentences are clear, complete, and relatively error free.

Final Project—Showcase Piece

Instructions

You will create a showcase piece to highlight what you've learned about writing about writing. The medium you select is your choice – you could do a video, a song, a poem, a short story, a painting…there are many possibilities. If you are considering an option not mentioned above, you must discuss your idea with me.

This showcase piece takes effort, time, and, especially, planning and critical thinking about what writing means to you. You might consider how to represent your initial views of writing and your current views. You might consider how to represent your view of writing and reading versus how others see those activities. You might consider representing what forms of writing and reading are valuable in your life. These are just some ideas to help you get started. Remember, you are flexing your creative muscles to think critically about writing, so be imaginative!

You should include a four- to six-page typed reflection essay discussing the significance of your showcase piece. Analyze what this piece represents to you about writing and connect your showcase to the issues we've discussed in the course. To make these connections, you'll quote from the readings, your essays, your reading responses, and maybe even class discussions. This essay should be cited using MLA style.

Evaluation Criteria

Entire project (presentation and essay) is based on a literacy model or based on the idea of a written work.

- The message of your literacy model is clearly conveyed to your audience in both the presentation and the essay, in whatever medium you choose.
- Presentation includes evidence or a physical text/song/poem/essay/video/painting component that represents the idea you want to convey in a clear way.
- Essay includes details about the presentation, explanation of how it represents literacy, and some reflection on the actual presentation.

Where We Are: The State of Digital Publishing in Rhetoric and Composition

This is the first installment of an occasional section of the journal, "Where We Are," which highlights where we are as a field on matters current and compelling. In these invited contributions, we bring together a small group of scholars at the forefront of a particular issue or practice, who together issue a progress report of sorts (in 800-1200 words!). Our next installment focuses on disability and accessibility, and will appear in Fall 42.2. –*Editor's Note*

New Realities for Scholarly Presses in Trying Economic Times

David Blakesley, Clemson University

About Parlor Press

Parlor Press is an independent publisher and distributor of scholarly and trade books in print and digital formats. It was founded in 2002 to address the need for an alternative scholarly, academic press attentive to emergent ideas and forms while maintaining the highest possible standards of quality, credibility, and integrity. Our primary and simple goal is to publish outstanding writing in a variety of subjects and thus to disseminate knowledge about writing and rhetoric as widely as possible and to ensure that this educational mission is met with style and grace. In my idealistic moments, I believe that people everywhere ought to know what we know (that it's rhetoric all the way down, for instance!) and that students can indeed be taught to write well.

Parlor Press's name comes from that Burkeian parlor we hear mentioned so often and embodies what Burke had in mind, a living example of the unending conversation of history into which we are borne. Imagine you enter a parlor, he wrote. You've come late. People are having a heated discussion about this and that. However, everyone arrives as you do, so no one is qualified to retrace all the steps that have come before. You listen for a while, then you put in your oar. People come to your defense or align themselves against you, and then you depart with the discussion still vigorously in progress (*Philosophy of Literary Form* 110-11). *Composition Studies* has graciously provided this forum for give-and-take in the parlor about (digital) publishing since we all have a stake in its future. This parlor—and Parlor Press, I hope—is a place where interesting and smart discussions come to the fore, where people speak (*parler* means "to speak," after all) and listen, where the dialogue and debate—the parliamentary—are in play. In the end, this is what all of our university presses want more than anything. Sometimes we believe they simply want to sell books and make money so that they can sell even more books. However, the ideal of most scholarly presses is to disseminate knowledge, with uncompromising concern for quality and currency. Only secondarily—and in more recent times—has it become necessary for presses to worry about the pedigrees of authors and the marketability of books (the other kind of currency). As John B. Thompson points out in his encyclopedic *Books in the Digital Age*, the golden age of university press publishing may have ended in the mid-1970s.

Tough economic times have exacerbated this downward trend, which continues to threaten all of our presses. Sales to libraries have dropped precipitously. Exhibiting at conferences is outrageously expensive. Return rates have risen dramatically. Yet the pressure on young scholars to publish books continues to mount, in spite of MLA's efforts to expose the crisis in scholarly publishing and to reject the monograph as the gold standard for promotion. At the same time, as our numbers increase and academic fields splinter into countless subspecialties, fewer and fewer people have time to read the major books published in their field. Thompson calls this the "twigging" effect (177). He also cites the troubling practice of tenure committees to abdicate their responsibilities to evaluate scholarship themselves and grant it to the presses without question, often merely on the basis of reputation or, more indirectly, the success of the university's football team. Thankfully, almost two dozen authors have earned tenure primarily on the basis of their Parlor Press books, which is gratifying.

What Now?

Parlor Press is independent of any university, although we do have many ongoing collaborative projects with universities, organizations, and journals around the world. We're managed entirely by scholars and writers in their respective fields, presently covering eighteen book series. The editors and I manage everything from initial peer review through production, distribution, and marketing. We have no staff or outside funding sources. It is all built on the sweat equity of enormously generous and wise editors who believe that we can make a difference and that, if left to our own devices and free of all bureaucratic machinery, we might find a way out of this mess and don't have to sell our souls to some conglomerate to do it. Meanwhile, we have ensured that our peer review process is rigorous, and development, deeply collaborative. Publication decisions are made by experts in the field, as they should be, and are impervious to marketing departments or corporate boards.

People frequently ask whether the whole operation, as complex as it is, has longevity and is sustainable. They started asking these questions in 2002. Here we are in 2014. The good news is that our funding hasn't been cut or threatened, if only because we have none to begin with (the glass is half full, I guess). Sales have risen steadily—from almost none to a number respectable enough to keep everything running smoothly and to maintain, as they say, our "growth mode." In twelve years, we have published 180 books involving more than 600 authors. Seventy-five books are under contract. This year, we will publish 25 more. We just launched three new series (Game Studies, edited by Cynthia Haynes and Jan Rune Holmevik; Violence and Popular Culture, edited by Philip Simpson; and Architectural Environments, edited by Akel Kahera and Craig Anz). Plans to single-source all of our books for delivery across print and all digital platforms, in ePub, Mobi, PDF, and iBook formats are nearly complete. Soon, we'll be delivering content via Adobe's Digital Publishing Suite in the form of an App that allows readers to access all content on a subscription basis for a very low price or in smaller units, a la Apple's iTunes Store. We're also venturing into the world of augmented reality with the Fall 2014 release of Sean Morey and John Tinnell's *Augmented Reality: Innovative Perspectives Across Art, Industry, and Academia*. We're now publishing or managing production and distribution for eight scholarly journals.

Parlor Press is a phenomenon made possible by what Chris Anderson in *The Long Tail* called the "democratization of production" (*passim*). It is also much easier to innovate when you've gone rogue. We have leveraged new digital printing and publishing technologies while also developing a sustainable model for managing all aspects of scholarly publishing efficiently and productively. The model takes advantage of, among other things, digital printing technologies (such as print-on-demand) and powerful communication technologies like Drupal for collaboration, content management, and production in a network of distributed responsibility. Scholars, organizations, and institutions with a clear stake in creative and scholarly research have managed to pool limited resources. We are in rhetoric and composition, after all. We're used to building grand designs from nothing but hard work.

What This Freedom Makes Possible

I'd like to mention a few examples of what this freedom makes possible. In a partnership with Mike Palmquist and the WAC Clearinghouse at Colorado State University—we created the first open-access book publishing project in our field (or any, perhaps) to offer free ebooks with a print option, the Reference Guides to Rhetoric and Composition series edited by Charles Bazerman.

Since then, we have published many more CC–licensed books in electronic and print formats, including the first in rhetoric and composition ever published under such a license, John Logie's *Peers, Pirates, and Persuasion*. The WAC Clearinghouse now also publishes the Perspectives on Writing series that releases books under a CC license with a print option fulfilled by Parlor Press. The print versions of these "free" books have sold every bit as well as our print-only books, if not better. In March 2014, we published *Invasion of the MOOCs: The Promises and Perils of Massive Open Online Courses*, edited by Steven Krause and Charles Lowe, under a CC license with a free PDF version and print option. The book was downloaded more than 4,000 times and sold more than 100 copies in its first two weeks. So, the innovation is there, and the future is bright if we can continue to find creative solutions for publishing our scholarly work.

What You Can Do

Here are some things you can do to ensure that scholarly publishing in rhetoric and composition thrives. I've cobbled these steps together from experience, friends, and fellow publishers, people like Lisa Bayer (Director, University of Georgia Press), Karl Kageff (Editor-in-Chief, Southern Illinois University Press), and Jonathan Haupt (Director, University of South Carolina Press). (I am proud to say that all of these fine people are former students of mine from SIU-Carbondale and are scholars in their own right in rhetoric and composition.)

1. Learn about scholarly presses in your field and especially those who publish in your specialty. Visit their websites and meet the publisher and editors at conferences. Learn what they do. Subscribe to their RSS feeds. Your knowledge will spread to others.
2. Read the work of colleagues, either by buying their books or asking your library to acquire them.
3. Encourage your associations and libraries to partner with scholarly presses (rather than only mega-presses and journal conglomerates) when publishing journals, books and other digital projects. If you're an editor, ask a press if it's interested in helping you publish your journal.
4. Buy and assign books from scholarly presses in your courses, which means taking the time to find out what they have published lately and what's coming down the pike.
5. Support the concept of intellectual property and author rights by discouraging the pirating of copyrighted books.
6. If you enjoy a press's free e-books, buy a printed one now and then, too.

7. Request that your university library purchase specific titles you believe are important to your field and research. Ask your library to put the press on its "buy list" with jobbers so that all new titles get ordered automatically. Forward all flyers from publishers to library acquisitions and ask them to buy. This step alone would be a huge boost for our publishers.

8. Give scholarly books to your friends as gifts.

9. Become a friend of your favorite university press. Donate money to a UP in tribute of your favorite scholar in the field on the occasion of his/her birthday.

10. Talk up your favorite or local scholarly press in conversations with colleagues and people in your community.

11. Do the research needed to find classic or cutting edge work by terrific scholars and/or public intellectuals in your field. Become a repeat adopter of one or more scholarly books. As an engaged teacher, you will enliven your students and help create the perennial bestsellers that university presses count on to survive.

12. If involved in planning a conference, treat the presses as colleagues in a common pursuit, not as simply "vendors."

13. Review scholarly books in journals. If our journals published reviews as frequently as *Composition Studies*, we'd be set.

14. Volunteer to help a press in some way. Also, don't be afraid to barter. Since much of "publishing" is made up of gratis academic labor, you can help a great deal and reap some benefit, if only free books.

15. Write letters to university administrators or others who might need to know how much you appreciate the work of the press or an editor. Be an independent lobbyist, in other words. Parlor Press has a number of great people who do this for us, and it's very important (and appreciated, believe me).

Conclusion

I could go on (there's so much to do!), but the hour grows late and it's time to depart, with the discussion still vigorously in progress.

Works Cited

Anderson, Chris. *The Long Tail: Why the Future of Business is Selling Less of More*. New York: Hyperion, 2006. Print.

Burke, Kenneth. *The Philosophy of Literary Form: Studies in Symbolic Action*. 1941. Berkeley: U of California P, 1973. Print.

Krause, Steven D., and Charles Lowe. *Invasion of the MOOCs: The Promises and Perils of Massive Open Online Courses*. Anderson: Parlor, 2014. Print.

Logie, John. *Peers, Pirates, and Persuasion: Rhetoric in the Peer-to-Peer Debates*. West Lafayette: Parlor, 2006. Print.

Morey, Sean, and John Tinnell. *Augmented Reality: Innovative Perspectives Across Art, Industry, and Academia*. Anderson: Parlor, 2014. Print.

Thompson, John B. *Books in the Digital Age: The Transformation of Academic and Higher Education Publishing in Britain and the United States*. Cambridge: Polity Press, 2005. Print.

Composing Change: The Role of Graduate Education in Sustaining a Digital Scholarly Future

Kristine L. Blair, Bowling Green State University

In "Reading the Archives: Ten Years on Nonlinear (*Kairos*) History," James Kalmbach acknowledges the significant role graduate students have played as digital innovators in the field, particularly in the formation of *Kairos: A Journal of Rhetoric, Technology, Pedagogy* in 1996. Graduate students in my own Rhetoric and Writing doctoral program at Bowling Green State University have displayed similar innovation in their editorial work on *Computers and Composition Online*, which I have been honored to edit since 2002. These are inspiring graduate student success stories within the profession, and certainly, there are others, such as the more recent graduate student development of the journal *Present Tense: A Journal of Rhetoric and Society*. Indeed, given the ever increasing and ever evolving role of digital tools in our students' literate lives inside and outside the classroom, it is vital that we question how graduate students, as future faculty, are trained not only to develop digital scholarly agendas but also to be similar change agents in both English Departments and writing programs. This change agent role is not an unfamiliar one to teacher-scholars working in computers and composition studies. We need only review the work of established scholars such as Cynthia Selfe and Gail Hawisher and their emphasis on the role of literacy narratives within and across cultures, or the equally powerful work of Cheryl Ball, the current editor of *Kairos*, and her ongoing advocacy for multimodal digital scholarship. As rapidly as technologies change, however, very often our questions and concerns remain the same. Thus despite the efforts of these and other innovative scholars, despite a changing academic job market in which digital media skills are increasingly prominent in position descriptions (Lauer, forthcoming), and despite the original graduate student editors of *Kairos* who paved the way for the rest of us, the numbers of graduate students in rhetoric and writing who actually develop the skill set to self-identify as multimodal literacy specialists remain limited. This has to change.

Enabling change in the future requires that we remember the lessons of the past. Perhaps the most important reminder is Cynthia Selfe's longstanding emphasis on "paying attention" to how contemporary literate and textual practices are "changing our understanding of what it means to be literate in the twenty-first century and help[ing] us understand our own role in relation to change" (Selfe 44). Selfe addresses multiple audiences, calling upon parents, teachers, and citizens to share responsibility in literacy education. Similarly, in the context of graduate students' emerging digital scholarly identities, there are a number of factors to which their advisors and mentors must pay attention and for which they should share responsibility:

Curriculum

As much as we advocate multimodality across the undergraduate writing curriculum, that goal is dependent on multimodality across the graduate curriculum in classrooms and in other professional development spaces. All too often the task of technological training is delegated to the single course, the single expert in the program, a technical role that earlier theorists have referred to as the "white coat syndrome" (Zeni). Yet graduate students must have consistent opportunities to "invent themselves in multimodality" (Journet), from the course in multimodal composing to the course in research methods, to understand the role that technology plays in teacher-researcher identity. To achieve this goal, we should encourage our students to grow as co-teachers and researchers, demonstrating the use of the latest literacy technologies in ways that teach us as much as we teach them. Equally important, this process extends beyond our classrooms and into collaborative, increasingly multimodal publication processes and editorial work on journals.

Genres and Modalities

In my own teaching and research, I have focused specifically on genres that allow students to experiment with digital identity, including eportfolios and digital dissertations, as well as on the material conditions of graduate student experience in determining the role visual and aural modes can play in data collection and data representation. How might these genres and modes represent professional development opportunities that prepare graduate students for roles as techno-rhetoricians? These genres represent starting points, crucial training grounds for future digital scholarship in both article and book form. Admittedly, such genres have had limited use value in English studies' continued privileging of the alphabetic literacies for not only the academic job market but also the research and publication process. Nevertheless, as technology advances more rapidly than policy, pedagogy, and ideology, our field faces a shift from the large screen to the small screen, and the resulting need to understand the range of template, design, and code literacies vital to the presentation of a digital scholarly self. As a digital writing teacher-researcher, I strongly believe these literacies foster an ownership and an investment among students that privileged conventions and genres of print academic discourse typically fail to encourage.

Politics

Even as I advocate change, the question is, as it has always been, how to keep up with that change. To that end, the technological education graduate students receive must inherently be a political education as they become faculty who both understand and inevitably reshape the values of the units in which they reside, including (1) the balance between alphabetic and multimodal literacies in research and teaching and (2) the standards by which these future faculty are themselves evaluated for tenure and promotion as they engage in digital scholarly production. Our students' current and future role as change agents requires them to educate faculty colleagues and administrative leaders about digital teaching and research through rhetorical modeling. In turn, my own role as a senior faculty member and department chair involves advocacy for pre-tenure colleagues in a range of committee, policy, and institutional settings.

As a graduate educator and online journal editor, I worry that our larger scholarly dialogues too narrowly focus on the limited number of nationally recognized digital writing programs with access to a wider range of institutional resources. Rather than reinscribe a divide between "the haves" and the "have-nots," more graduate programs in the field should view the digital literacy acquisition of graduate students as a shared responsibility among colleagues that includes the students themselves in a reciprocal, recursive mentoring model that will shape their future faculty identities, online and off. It is this model that has led to the success of *Computers and Composition Online*, with graduate students serving as section editors, working with prospective web authors on both content and design issues, and gaining experience in all aspects of the digital editorial workflow. While such activities sustain both a future for digital scholarly publishing and our inevitable relevance as a discipline devoted to literacy education, they also enable a technological and ideological identity shift among our students as they remind others, and as Selfe has before them, to "pay attention" to change in the 21st century.

Works Cited

Kalmbach, James. "Reading the Archives: Ten Years on Nonlinear (*Kairos*) History." *Kairos: A Journal of Rhetoric, Technology, and Pedagogy* 11.1 (2011): n. pag. Web. 15 Mar. 2014. <http://kairos.technorhetoric.net/11.1/binder.html?topoi/kalmbach/index.html>.

Lauer, Claire. "Expertise With New/Multi/Modal/Visual/Digital/Media Technologies Desired: Tracing Composition's Evolving Relationship With Technology Through The MLA JIL." *Computers and Composition* (forthcoming). Print.

Journet, Debra. "Inventing Myself In Multimodality: Encouraging Senior Faculty To Use Digital Media." *Computers and Composition* 24.2 (2007): 107-20. Print.

Selfe, Cynthia L. *Technology And Literacy In The 21ˢᵗ Century: The Importance Of Paying Attention*. Carbondale: SIUP, 1999. Print.

Selfe, Cynthia L. "Students Who Teach Us: A Case Study Of A New Media Text Designer." *Writing New Media: Theory and Applications for Expanding the Teaching of Composition*. Anne Frances Wysocki, Johndan Johnson-Eilola, Cynthia L. Selfe, and Geoffrey Sirc. Logan: Utah State UP, 2004. 44-66. Print.

Zeni, Jane. "Literacy, Technology, and Teacher Education." *Literacy And Computers: The Complications Of Teaching And Learning With Technology*. Ed. Cynthia L. Selfe and Susan Hilligoss. New York: MLA, 1994. 76-88. Print.

Evolving Digital Publishing Opportunities Across Composition Studies

Gail E. Hawisher, University of Illinois, Urbana-Champaign
Cynthia L. Selfe, The Ohio State University

Since the early 1980s, the profession has seen plenty of changes in the arena of digital scholarly publishing: during this time, while the specific challenges have seldom remained the same, the presence and the pressures of rapid technological change endure. In fact, as an editorial team that has, in part, focused on digital publishing, we've come to recognize *change* as a constant companion that serves to shape our scholarly lives in exciting, albeit unpredictable, ways. In this essay, we map some of the major publishing challenges that have presented themselves to our field over the last thirty years and speculate on possible challenges that might characterize the future of digital scholarly publishing in composition studies. We hasten to point out that our view is only one snapshot of current and past digital publishing contexts and that others in this section of *Composition Studies* present valuable perspectives to add to our own.

Early Publishing Challenges

To begin, and, by way of background, we note that during the 1980s, academic print journals and presses in rhetoric and composition accepted only a very few pieces about digital composition for publication. Editors were sometimes perplexed over the digital nature of scholarship, and journals, for the most part, focused on the production, analysis, and evaluation of alphabetic texts. Thus, we began our editorship together by creating a new academic journal, *Computers and Composition*[1] and, in 1989, by coediting scholarly collections like *Critical Perspectives on Computers and Composition,* with different contributors, collaborators, and colleagues. In these endeavors—and the others we recount below—we sought to provide publication venues for those working on digital media and writing and to promote colleagues' and graduate students' scholarly efforts at a time when they were receiving little recognition.

In such efforts, collaboration was often essential to publication for digital scholars. Collaborative approaches also enlarged the collective vision of rhetoric and composition with cutting-edge publications while at the same time supporting scholars—colleagues and graduate students—who claimed digital composition as their own. In our own case, to sustain both the production of scholarly texts and ongoing editorial projects, the collaborative efforts of

Composition Studies 42.1 (2014): 107–113

graduate students at Illinois, Michigan Tech, Ohio State, and other universities, including Purdue, Virginia Tech, and the University of Massachusetts, Amherst, among them, became essential. These students contributed as editors and bibliographers, as authors and co-authors; they helped create and edit articles and journals and edited collections. This hands-on approach to scholarly production and editing, we believe, resulted in projects that brought a large cadre of graduate students across the country together as colleagues—often using digital contexts to communicate—and encouraged them to initiate their own publications as well. Such collaborative projects also functioned to focus the attention of the larger profession on the scholarly community working in computers and composition as an emerging area of literacy studies and to argue for the importance of this scholarship.

Challenges of Publishing in a Digital World Continue

As print publications in composition studies became more open to digital scholarship over the next decades, however, digital scholars began to chaff at the limitations of print and print publications, recognizing that the two-dimensional printed page often constrained the representation of linguistic phenomena, the reporting of data, the investigatory voices of both digital and nondigital scholars in unacknowledged ways. Thus, in recent decades, some scholars in rhetoric and composition have focused on finding outlets in which to publish *born digital* work. With the term "born digital," we refer to publications made expressly for digital communication that are not simply transformations from paper to digital environments. Indeed there is nothing simple about well-crafted born digital text productions. By the 1990s, *Kairos*, *CCC Online*, the *WAC Clearinghouse*, and *C&C Online* were created to provide outlets for born digital works that merited attention alongside articles in print journals.

These new venues published texts that incorporated mediated elements within article-length scholarship often characterized as "multimodal" (although multimodal can refer, of course, to print texts such as illuminated manuscripts, illustrated books, and more). As Kathleen Fitzpatrick explains in *Planned Obsolescence*:

> What is it that I mean when I say 'multimodal' . . . when my computer translates my words into the very same substance that sound, image, and other modes of representation exist in, we encounter the potential for a radical change, asking us to consider what a text is, what it can be, in the digital age. (27)

Although Fitzpatrick describes born digital texts and published an early example of such a text, she stops just short here of arguing how such texts might fulfill scholarly requirements for job security. This challenge continues to grow as scholarship moves off the printed page onto the screen.

In related ways during this same period, the challenges of publishing born digital scholarly works with the same specific gravity of books—rather than articles—also assumed growing importance. Although university presses diminished in numbers, and print publications grew increasingly expensive to produce, departments of English continued to perceive books and monographs as the "gold standard" (Task Force 10) for tenure and promotion in many institutions.

In 2007 as an experiment in confronting these challenges, we established Computers and Composition Digital Press (CCDP), which soon became an imprint of Utah State University Press. Formed as a nonprofit entity, CCDP published born digital book projects, although they assumed different forms and genres. Since its inception, CCDP has published nine such projects in an open access, peer reviewed, and online environment, many of which have played important roles in establishing their authors' credentials within their departments and across the field. (See http://ccdigitalpress.org/ebooks-and-projects for a list of CCDP publications.) The goal of the press is to honor the traditional academic values of rigorous peer review and intellectual excellence but also to combine this work with a commitment to innovative digital scholarship and expression. For CCDP editors,[2] the press represents an important kind of scholarly activism—an effort to respond to changing publishing environments by circulating the best work of digital media scholars in a timely fashion and on the global scale made possible through digital distribution. The work of the press has been recognized with several important awards: the CCCC Best Book Award (2013), Advancement in Knowledge Award (2013), Research Impact Award (2013), as well as the Coalition of Women Scholars' Outstanding Book Award (2012) and the C&C Distinguished Book Award at the 2013 Computers and Writing Conference. Each of these awards, we believe, illustrates the potential of born digital books to achieve a well-earned reputation for excellence.[3]

The work of CCDP continues to depend, to a great extent, on collaborative endeavors. Heidi McKee and Dànielle DeVoss's born digital edited collection, *Digital Writing: Assessment and Evaluation*, includes the work of forty-one different authors and eleven multiauthor teams. This collection also takes a born-digital form in which mediated elements are not add-ons. As James Kalmbach points out, readers find themselves moving fluidly back and forth between argument and multimodal examples . . . in a way that feels totally natural and appropriate. *Digital Writing: Assessment and Evaluation* is the first book-length online project I have reviewed in which its born-digital nature feels essential to its argument.

We find it revealing too, as James Purdy and Joyce Walker point out, that when we turn to tenure and promotion discussions that involve digital publications, conversations often "focus primarily on establishing digital work as equivalent to print publications . . . instead of considering how digital scholarship might transform knowledge-making practices" (178).

In our own thinking, of course, digital scholarly publications have the potential for this kind of important intellectual work. So, given the current state of scholarly publishing in composition studies, what are the possible vectors that might characterize future challenges?

The Continuing and Accelerating Pace of Change

We see no evidence that the pace or extent of change will slow in digital scholarly publishing. Given new digital tools and protocols, software and hardware, genres and expectations, we see only an acceleration of change. As a result presses like CCDP should remain wide open to experimentation and to entering members of the profession for imaginative solutions to problems.

While print presses deal with proofreaders and copyeditors, fulfillment and warehousing, indexing and binding, paper and reproduction costs, CCDP has been able to establish editorial positions that are less frequently encountered in contemporary print publishing: among them, CCDP Senior Editors work to establish a system for ensuring that our born digital projects are cataloged by the Library of Congress and that online published projects are revised on a regular basis as formats inevitably change (Patrick Berry, Syracuse University); to identify approaches for digital accessibility (Melanie Yergeau, University of Michigan); to guide us toward the newest shared protocols for multimedia authoring and digital circulation (Timothy Lockridge, Miami University). We have also asked Blog Editors (Ryan Trauman, Columbia College, and Harley Ferris, University of Louisville) to create and edit blogs related to CCDP publications; established a Social Media and Visibility Editor (Amber Buck, College of Staten Island); a Technological Development Editor (Derek Van Ittersum, Kent State University); and an Authors' Manual Editor (Quinn Warnock, Virginia Tech University) to produce a dynamic online reference for publishing with CCDP.

Collaborations and Partnerships

Although new digital presses like CCDP promise exciting new genres of born digital projects, these publications are not easy to compose or produce. Indeed, we have found that such publications often require massive amounts of cooperation and various kinds of collaborative team efforts involving humanist scholars and programmers; established scholars, junior scholars, and graduate students; and more. Providing appropriate credit for such large-scale efforts in tenure and promotion cases further challenge and resist the historical conception of the single-authored book. We also believe that collaborative partnerships between emerging born digital presses and farsighted university presses, such as Utah State University Press (under the leadership of Michael Spooner) with established reputations, routes of circulation, and editorial procedures are productive ways of dealing with the rapidly changing landscapes of scholarly publishing.

Preparation and Education

With the changing set of challenges that face digital publishing, educating composition scholars to compose only alphabetic texts (or to analyze them, assess them, or circulate them) is a disservice. We will all need to read and compose and exchange new kinds of texts, and our changing scholarship will demand new mediated genres. One recent CCDP project, *Stories that Speak to Us* (Eds. H. Lewis Ulman, Scott L. DeWitt, Cynthia L. Selfe) is a set of multimedia curated exhibits rather than chapters, a collection that is part database, part archive, part scholarly text, part social-media composition. It is both book and nonbook, an example of "convergence culture" in Henry Jenkins's words, within which mediated forms and possibilities come together to make new kinds of meaning. The concept of "author" or "editor" in such projects, clearly, is inadequate to the task of describing the effort involved in composing or publishing.

Changing Landscapes, Nimble Responses

The extent of the changes we have outlined is not likely to diminish in the near future; changes in digital communication technologies touch all aspects of publishing as a complex set of cultural phenomena. As university presses continue to struggle in terms of fiscal resources, and as born digital projects place increasing demands on scholars, editors, and presses, systems of academic peer review are also changing profoundly in digital environments (Fitzpatrick; Selfe and Hawisher). Changing technological environments exert pressures on the time allocated to the reviewing process; the anonymity and format of reviews; reviewing as labor and reviews as scholarly contributions, even on the public circulation and incorporation of reviewers' comments. In confronting such challenges, small nonprofit presses like CCDP position themselves best when they are flexible and nimble. For us, this means, in part, foregoing economic returns that both support and constrain the efforts of for-profit presses.

Writing in 2014, Jeremy Dyehouse reminds us of Richard Ohmann's prescient 1985 argument of the danger of "technological determinism" even as we recount here some of the transformative possibilities of digital publication. As Dyehouse puts it, "Ohmann cautioned against deterministic thinking about computer technologies, which were then—as now—described as poised to transform life and learning" (262). Digital publication cannot transform our academic lives, but it must receive its due. Until we have publishing venues that regularly feature digital texts—that have the potential to count for job security alongside their print counterparts—scholars will have difficulty with the new meanings and identities that people continually assemble and reassemble through language, literate exchange, digital media, and the texts of academic living.

Notes

1. *Computers and Composition* was founded by Kate Kiefer and Cynthia Selfe in 1983 and began its tenure as an international journal when Gail Hawisher joined Selfe in the editorship in 1988.

2. See http://ccdigitalpress.org/about/editors-bios for current list of editors.

3. A listing of awards includes Susan Delagrange's *Technologies of Wonder* (2013 CCCC Best Book Award); Patrick W. Berry, Gail E. Hawisher, and Cynthia L. Selfe's *Transnational Literate Lives* (2013 CCCC Advancement in Knowledge Award and 2013 CCCC Research Impact Award); Delagrange's *Technologies of Wonder* (2012 Winifred Bryan Horner Book Award for the *Coalition of Women Scholars* in the History of Rhetoric and Composition); and Debra Journet, Cheryl Ball, and Ryan Trauman's edited *The New Work of Composing* (2012 *Computers and Composition* Distinguished Book Award).

Works Cited

Dyehouse, Jeremiah. "Theory in the Archives: Fred Newton Scott and John Dewey on Writing the Social Organism." *College English* 76.3 (2014): 248-68. Print.

Fitzpatrick, Kathleen. *Planned Obsolescence: Publishing, Technology, and the Future of the Academy.* New York: New York UP, 2011. Web. 30 December 2013.

Hawisher, Gail E., and Cynthia L. Selfe. *Critical Perspectives on Computers and Composition Instruction.* New York: Columbia U Teachers Coll. P, 1989. Print.

Jenkins, Henry. *Convergence Culture: Where Old and New Media Collide.* New York: New York UP, 2008. Print.

Kalmbach, James. Review. McKee, Heidi, and Dànielle Nicole Devoss, eds. *Digital Writing: Assessment and Evaluation.* Logan, UT: Computers and Composition

Digital P/Utah State UP, 2013. Web. 14 Feb. 2014. <http://ccdigitalpress.org/ebooks-and-projects/dwae#reviews>.

McKee, Heidi, and Dànielle Nicole Devoss, eds. *Digital Writing: Assessment and Evaluation*. Logan, UT: Computers and Composition Digital P/Utah State UP, 2013. Web. 14 Feb. 2014. <http://ccdigitalpress.org/dwae/index.html>.

MLA Task Force on Evaluating Scholarship for Tenure and Promotion. "Report of the MLA Task Force on Evaluating Scholarship for Tenure and Promotion." *Profession* (2007): 9-71. *MLA*. Web. 30 December 2013.

Purdy, James P., and Joyce R. Walker. "Valuing Digital Scholarship: Exploring the Changing Realities of Intellectual Work." *Profession* (2010): 177-95. Print.

Selfe, Cynthia L., and Gail E. Hawisher. "Methodologies of Peer and Editorial Review: Changing Practices." *CCC* 63.4 (2012): 672-98. Print.

Ulman, H. Louis, Scott Lloyd DeWitt, and Cynthia L. Selfe, eds. *Stories That Speak to Us: Exhibits from the Digital Archives of Literacy Narratives*. Logan, UT: Computers and Composition Digital P/Utah State UP, 2013. Web. 14 Feb. 2014. <http://ccdigitalpress.org/stories/>.

Composing for Digital Publication: Rhetoric, Design, Code

Douglas Eyman, George Mason University
Cheryl E. Ball, West Virginia University

W e begin our discussion of the state of digital publication with the claim that, at this historical moment, nearly all composition is digital composition. But, as a field, composition studies has not yet made that shift completely explicit in our discussions of composing processes and writing pedagogies. A deeper engagement with this very rapid shift in modes, genres, and media of textual production is not only warranted but critical for build-ing literacies and research in writing and writing studies. Part of the reason for this lack of digital literacy development may be that the rationale for add-ing multiple literacies in design and code—areas traditionally not considered part of our fields of expertise—needs to be more clearly stated in order to be considered as part of the foundations—the infrastructures—of composing (DeVoss, Cushman, & Grabill). Based on our nearly two decades of work with *Kairos*, we posit that the infrastructural considerations for digital com-posing in the form of webtext publishing include

- the *scholarly* (whether a disciplinary field allows/values webtexts),
- the *social* (how a field or journal behaves when implementing those values within the publishing process), and
- the *technical* (whether and how systems support the perpetuity of scholarly and social infrastructures). (Eyman & Ball)

But these considerations are difficult to concretely include in classroom prac-tice, so we offer three critical practices for composition that accommodate the many media, modes, and delivery mechanics in use today: rhetoric, design, and code.

Rhetoric

In many ways, the rhetorical dimensions of digital texts are no different from those of print or oral texts—all of which require attention to the rhetorical situation (the purpose and argument forwarded by the writer/performer/de-signer, the needs and expectations of the audience, and the overall sociocul-tural context of the communication, regardless of medium). For born-digital webtexts that engage multiple modes and media as a function of their genre, additional rhetorical concerns arise with regard to decisions about delivery, access(ability), and sustainability. Authors of webtexts need to ask themselves: is this work best presented in a more linguistically rich (written) or visually rich (images, layout, video, etc.) format? To what degree does interaction help to express the argument? Is an audio component necessary for this particular form? Etc. It is critical for webtext designers to consider the ramifications of these decisions on the relative *use, usability,* and *usefulness* of their text: "use" focuses on how the audience/user will make use of the webtext or digital object; "usability" speaks to the degree to which the users' needs have been taken into account in the design of a text; and "usefulness" (in the academic context) is tied to the disciplinary networks in which a text is designed to circulate (that is, to what extent is it useful to readers?). A text that is usable but not useful will be unsuccessful, just as texts that are useful but not usable are also unsuccessful. Authors must consider all three aspects when designing digital texts.

Design

Discussing design as a rhetorical move still feels fairly new in our field, despite scholars' previous discussions of design-as-rhetoric (Buchanan; Sheppard; Wysocki) and webtextual journals such as *Kairos* and *Computers & Composition Online* publishing designed scholarship for almost 20 years. How can our field—in our scholarship, our classes, our conferences—move toward design as integral to our arguments and as part of our invention processes? Design is a rhetorical function that plays an important role in each of the canons of rhetoric, most obviously related to style (particularly in terms of visual rhetoric), but also of organization. Instead of saying what design *is*, most design theorists describe what design *does*. Donald Norman describes how design should function, arguing that it should make conceptual models visible, including showing required or alternative actions and their possible results, and should do so easily and naturally for the user (187). These design approaches are easily applicable to physical and digital objects: Webtext authors embrace design so that the conceptual model they use is relevant to the text's purpose and media. (See also Kuhn, Johnson, and Lopez's description of *conceptual core*.) The challenge is to see texts (even word-processed texts) as objects that require design.

At *Kairos*, we embrace design as part of the invention process through our (pedagogically informed) mentorship of authors in pre-submission collaborations and through our collaborative peer review process (Ball). We then edit their designs (including the code, as needed) for sustainability, accessibility, usability, and readability. All of these are rhetorical concerns: an author who chooses to design her piece in Adobe Flash chooses a limited set of sustainable, accessible, usable, and readable features that may change over time, or even disappear (see Sorapure). These design choices function as part of a webtext's scholarly and technical infrastructures as well as part of the social infrastructure of *Kairos*'s collaborative authorial and editorial workflows.

Code

Code is the underlying structure that has to function properly in order for a digital text to achieve its design goals and support the rhetorical functions of usability and accessibility. Code is, in a way, analogous to grammar—in order to function properly it needs to adhere to certain standards: it must be well-formed and conform to a formal register that is (generally) enforced by the systems that interpret and execute the code. Code is also the underlying infrastructure that both drives interactivity and sets constraints on possible user actions, and in this way code is intimately tied to design and rhetoric. The features of code that bind the webtext and set the parameters for use map onto what Ian Bogost (2011) has described as procedural rhetorics; that is, the rhetorical functions enacted at the level of code that promote certain user activity over other possibilities. As such, it is equally important for authors of digital texts to understand and engage with the coding aspects of a webtext with as much rigor as the rhetorical and design aspects.

In pedagogical terms, code need not be equated with programming; indeed, most work with code for digital composition that we edit in *Kairos* takes the form of markup such as HTML. Coding as literate practice also includes knowledge of appropriate file formats and technical infrastructure, such as knowing which graphic formats are most effective for a given image, which encoding schemes will be most usable for delivering audio and video via the Web, and the importance of including transcripts and technical devices that ensure accessibility to the greatest number of users. We also consider metadata as related to coding because it is typically inserted into digital texts at the level of code rather than integrated visually into the text itself. The active construction of metadata should be a compositional practice because it is emblematic of the ways an author deploys rhetoric, design, and code as the means by which a given webtext engages scholarly, social, and technical infrastructure (see also Bono, Hisayasu, Sayers, and Wilson).

Webtext authors (and, by virtue of the digital nature of text production, *all* authors) need to fully respond to all three of layers of digital composing— rhetoric, design, and code—in order to craft effective, persuasive arguments. Our charge to the readers of *Composition Studies*, then, is to consider the ways in which our scholarly work, our research, and our pedagogical practices could support all three elements. And once you do that, we expect you to send us more great work to publish in *Kairos*.

Works Cited

Ball, Cheryl. "Multimodal Revision Techniques in Webtexts." *Classroom Discourse* 5.1 (2014): 91-105. Print.

Bogost, Ian. *Persuasive Games: The Expressive Power of Videogames.* Cambridge: MIT, 2011. Print.

Bono, J. James, Curtis Hisayasu, Jentery Sayers, and Matthew W. Wilson. "Standards in the Making: Composing with Metadata in Mind." *The New Work of Composing.* Ed. Debra Journet, Cheryl E. Ball, and Ryan Trauman. Logan: Computers and Composition Digital P/Utah State UP, 2012. N. pag. Web. 15 Mar. 2014. <http://ccdigitalpress.org/nwc/chapters/wilson-et-al/>.

Buchanan, Richard. "Declaration by Design: Rhetoric, Argument, and Demonstration in Design Practice." *Design Issues* 2.1 (1985): 4-22. Print.

DeVoss, Dànielle Nicole, Ellen Cushman, and Jeff Grabill. "Infrastructure and Composing: The When of New-Media Writing." *College Composition and Communication* 57.1 (2005): 14-44. Print.

Eyman, Douglas, and Cheryl Ball. "Digital Humanities Scholarship and Electronic Publication." *Rhetoric and the Digital Humanities.* Ed. Jim Ridolfo and William Hart-Davidson. Chicago: U of Chicago P, forthcoming 2014. Print.

Kuhn, Virginia, DJ Johnson, and David Lopez. "Speaking with Students: Profiles in Digital Pedagogy." *Kairos: A Journal of Rhetoric, Technology, and Pedagogy* 14.2 (2010): n. pag. Web. 15 Mar. 2014. <http://kairos.technorhetoric.net/14.2/interviews/kuhn/index.html>.

Norman, Donald. *The Design ff Everyday Things.* New York: Basic, 2002. Print.

Sheppard, Jennifer. "The Rhetorical Work of Multimedia Production Practices: It's More Than Just Technical Skill." *Computers and Composition* 26.2 (2009): 122-31. Print.

Sorapure, Madeleine. "Text, Image, Code, Comment: Writing in Flash." *Computers and Composition* 23.4 (2006): 412-29. Print.

Wysocki, Anne Frances. "Impossibly Distinct: On Form/Content and Word/Image in Two Pieces of Computer-Based Interactive Multimedia." *Computers and Composition* 18.2 (2001): 137-62. Print.

Scholars | Digital Representation | Publishing

Justin Hodgson, Indiana University

"Have your students made TheJUMP?" I asked this question back in 2009 with the launch of the *The Journal for Undergraduate Multimedia Projects* (*TheJUMP*).[1] It was a promotional ploy, to be sure, but it was a question with more significance than mere publicity: I was (and continue to be) genuinely interested in how many of us have made the jump to incorporating digital rhetoric and/or multimodal composition into our courses. The reason: if we are teaching multimedia "writing," then multimedia "writing" practices have likely made it into our own writerly activities. For rarely, it seems, do we teach things in which we have absolutely no experience; and as scholars and teachers, our "experiencing" typically takes shape in one of three ways: projects of the personal, pedagogical, and professional variety.

For me, this is where understanding the current state of digital publishing begins, as digital publishing is grounded as much in the "how" of scholars' producing as the "what" of publishers' publishing. What we are dealing with, then, is an attempt to account for changes in our mediating technologies. Despite the predictions of literary scholar and media theorist Friedrich Kittler, the digital (as apparatus, as culture, as medial integration) didn't efface mediation; rather, it led to a radical increase in the number, type, and degree of mediating practices. What this means, as Clay Shirky has argued, is that we can now do more and say more in more ways than ever before in human history. As our modes, methods, media, and mechanisms of expression mutate in newer and newer digital forms (rendering old practices in new ways, new practices in old ways, and new practices in new ways), we find ourselves at a moment where we create, critique, collaborate, and comment according to new and often unprecedented protocols. As such, scholars and publishers deal less with issues of "making public," or sharing/distributing scholarly works, and more with new techniques, perhaps even new techné, for scholarly production. These considerations introduce the need for new cognitive structures, explanatory models, and guiding practices, as well as illuminate old wounds (e.g., revisiting and refocusing issues of access).

Paradigms, Things, and Performance

Lev Manovich told us, back in 2001, that what we are dealing with is an emergent "new computer culture" (46)—the result of computer and culture coming together and introducing all manner of new manifestations and practices. But what, might we ask, would (or do) these new manifestations look like? If new modes of representation usher in new modes of expression, argumentation, analysis and interpretation, and so on, then how are we to account for them? That is, if new modes of representation open scholarly practices to new potentialities, and if digital publishing provides ways for showcasing and validating that work, then it might serve us well to take stock of these changes.

Operating from a kind of paradigmatic scale, Gregory L. Ulmer's corpus, which both predates and postdates Manovich, introduces us to a new genre (mystory), a new methodology (CATTt), a new mode of reason (conductive logic), a new form/type of civic engagement (egent consultancy), and even a new term for the entire apparatus: *electracy*.[2] Ulmer offers his neologism to help shift us out from under literacy imperatives (e.g., computer literacy, digital literacy, multimedia literacy, etc.), which limit our understandings of emerging mediascapes. Further, his electrate practices (like the mystory projects published in *TheJUMP* and *Kairos*) orchestrate new relationships among readers and writers and raise different intensities and patterns for response. What this points us toward, however, is not necessarily any particular idiosyncrasy of Ulmer, but rather the openness of digital publishing to accommodate new forms, practices, and performances, each of which raise new (and often critical) considerations of accessibility practices, archiving strategies, and even audience responses and/or expectations.

Working from a decidedly different perspective, we might see how object-oriented composition practices are also asking for other kinds of digital publishing potentialities. Here, Jody Shipka's work comes to mind. Informed by the work of Bruno Latour, Shipka works to get her students to be cognitively aware of the fact that we are "always already collaborating with things" and, as a result, we are always already "working with or against the agency of things" ("Negotiating" W357). Picking this up from an ecological perspective, we might see that writing is, in whatever form, a distributed practice (see Edbauer, "Unframing"; Syverson) that functions in the interconnectedness of different types and degrees of agency. Thus, we might ask how digital publishing would shift if we start writing/producing with objects in radically different ways? If we take as an example one of the more memorable projects Shipka writes about in *Toward a Composition Made Whole*, where a student of hers transcribes an essay onto a pair of pink ballet shoes (2), we have to wonder how something like that could be "published." Of course, an object-oriented expression like ballet shoes may be a matter more pressing for the digital publishing of tomorrow, but with 3D printing quickly moving into the price range of general consumers, some of these authoring practices may not be too far afield.

Nonetheless, what Shipka's student example and the object-orientation suggest are, perhaps, a greater relationship moving forward between scholarly expression and things. And perhaps what is becoming of greater significance is not the artifact itself but the publishing moment: i.e., the performance (and its moment) for "making public" one's work. In Shipka's case, the ballet shoe was tied to a pedagogical moment, a classroom assignment, but I can't help but extend this thinking of "things" to *installation* and *performance* more generally. We've seen examples of things, installations, and performance all coming together in Victor Vitanza's *CCCC* and *MLA* galleria sessions[3], and we've seen conference presentations that were performances as well,[4] but there are yet other kinds of digital performances we might consider. Take, for example, the interactive installation by Kevin Brock and Dave Reider at the 2012 *CCCC* in St. Louis, MO. Using the Microsoft Kinect device, Brock and Reider set up a section of hallway in the convention center to act as interactive space (defined by the viewable area of the Kinect device). Passersby (and lingering participants like myself) found their silhouettes cast onto the wall in front of them: the negative space of their figuration populated with a live twitter feed from the conference. While this example doesn't fit neatly into any traditional molds of digital publishing, it was, nonetheless, a digital creation made public in both critical and scholarly ways. As such, we must account, to at least a minimal degree, for the act of digital performance. And while the artifact itself no longer remains, for its conference moment has passed, it lives on in blog posts, articles, video interviews, and the like—all offering testimonies to the performance and its significance, and, via their very existence, validating the work. In this case, "revisit-ability" is not the driving element of scholarly value; rather, the digital functions as part of the medium of the project itself as well as an apparatus (via networked technologies and platforms) for offering testimony.

Conclusion

What we might glean from this fly-by snippet of considerations is that the forms, products, and performances of digital scholarship are asking us to consider an entirely different set of artifacts, practices, and possibilities. And many of these considerations result from work that is "born digital" (Freidberg), meaning that digital scholarship today seems less and less multimediated versions of a priori textual articles, and instead is the result of actually writing/thinking with the affordances of new means and modes of representation. These practices, in turn, introduce (and call for) new techniques, new tropes, new techno-ontological conditions. Whether working with Ulmer's electrate paradigm, Shipka's object-composition, or Brock and Reider's installation, we see any number of different concepts and practices that have much to offer how we think about, create, and experience digital scholarship. Thus, with the new modes and means of representation and, more specifically, with the way scholars can manipulate those elements to offer us new insights on our ways of knowing, doing, and making the world, digital publishing is opening avenues to the latest aesthetics, ethics, and rhetorics we champion.

Notes

1. Launch video can be viewed on *TheJUMP* YouTube channel at https://www.youtube.com/watch?v=nroX9EMV2vE

2. For mystory, see Ulmer's *Teletheory* and *Internet Invention*. For his CATTt methodology, see *Heuretics: The Logic of Invention*. For his work on egents, the fifth estate, and consultancy, see *Electronic Monuments*. Collectively, all his works inform his construction of electracy, which is not only a felt-text created from electronic discourses and elements of the Derridean trace, but quite specifically is meant to have both resonances with and distinctions from literacy as a conceptual apparatus, paradigm, and practice.

3. In 2006, at the *Conference of College Composition and Communication*, Victor Vitanza coordinated the "Panel to Gallery" session, which was later curated by Virginia Kuhn and Vitanza and published as "From Gallery to Webtext" in *Kairos* 12.3. In 2012, Vitanza coordinated a similar event for the *Modern Language Association*, titled "MoMLA: From Gallery to Webtext," which was modeled on the "Medialounge" of the Museum of Modern Art in New York City. These too were edited into a collection by Vitanza and Kuhn and published in *Kairos* 17.2.

4. I'm thinking of Daniel Anderson's performance at the 2012 *Computers and Writing* conference where he played his MacBook Pro (and its media) like a pianist plays a Baby Grand—orchestrating videos, soundscapes, voice-overs, and so on in real time.

Work Cited

Collamati, Anthony. *Camera Creatures: Rhetorics of Light and Emerging Media*. Diss. Clemson U, 2011. Ann Arbor: UMI, 2011. Print.

Edbauer, Jenny. "Unframing Models of Public Distribution: From Rhetorical Situation to Rhetorical Ecologies." *RSQ* 35.4 (Fall 2005): 5-24. Print.

Edbauer Rice, Jenny. "Rhetoric's Mechanics: Retooling the Equipment of Writing Production." *CCC* 60.2 (Dec. 2008): 366-87. Print.

Friedberg, Anne. "On Digital Scholarship." *Cinema Journal* 48.2 (Winter 2009): 150-54. Print.

Kuhn, Virginia, and Victor J. Vitanza, Curators. "From Gallery to Webtext." *Kairos: A Journal of Rhetoric, Technology, and Pedagogy* 12.3 (2008): n. pag. Web. 10 Feb. 2014. <http://kairos.technorhetoric.net/12.3/topoi/gallery/index.html>.

Shipka, Jody. "Negotiating Rhetorical, Material, Methodological, and Technological Difference: Evaluating Multimodal Designs." *CCC* 61.1 (Sept. 2009): W343-66. Web.

—. *Toward a Composition Made Whole*. Pittsburgh: U of Pittsburgh P, 2011. Print.

Shirky, Clay. "How Social Media Can Make History." *TEDtalk*. June 2011. Video. Retrieved at www.ted.com.

Syverson, Margaret A. *The Wealth of Reality: An Ecology of Composition*. Carbondale: SIUP, 1999. Print.

Ulmer, Gregory L. *Electronic Monuments*. Minneapolis: U of Minnesota P, 2005. Print.

—. *Heuretics: The Logic of Invention*. Baltimore: The Johns Hopkins UP, 1994. Print.

—. *Internet Invention: From Literacy to Electracy*. New York: Longman, 2003. Print.

—. *Teletheory: Grammatology in the Age of Video*. New York: Routledge, 1989. Reprinted: Atropos Press, 2004. Print.

Vitanza, Victor J., and Virginia Kuhn, eds. "MoMLA: From Panel to Gallery." *Kairos: A Journal of Rhetoric, Technology, and Pedagogy* 17.2 (2013): n. pag. Web. 10 Feb. 2014. <http://www.technorhetoric.net/17.2/topoi/vitanza-kuhn/>.

Argumentation, Authority, and Accessibility in Digital Publishing: A Retrospective on *Composition Forum*

Christian Weisser, Penn State University, Berks
Kevin Brock, University of South Carolina

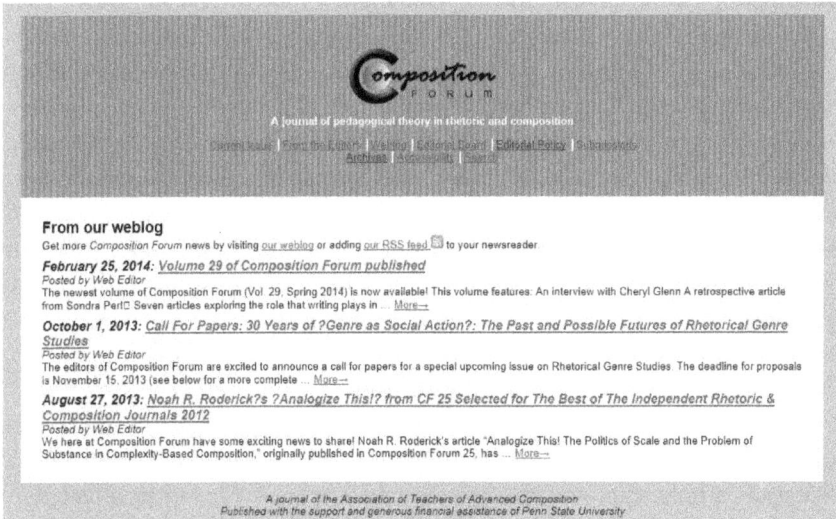

Introduction

The last decade has been an exciting time for electronic scholarly publication, especially in composition and rhetoric, where digital media experimentation has coincided with a rapidly increasing engagement with multimedia and multimodal composition. However, the field's embrace of electronic publication has been neither universal nor uniform. What has complicated this acceptance? The philosophy behind *Composition Forum*, a journal that has been published online and open-access since 2005, may provide an answer.

Composition Forum was first published in 1989 as a traditional print format peer-reviewed scholarly journal. At the time, electronic journals were still in their formative stages; most sources suggest that the first peer-reviewed electronic journal was not published until 1992 (Harter and Kim). From the outset, *Composition Forum* was intended as a medium for "scholars and teachers interested in the investigation of composition theory and its relation to the teaching of writing at the post-secondary level" ("Editorial Policy"). That focus has not changed significantly in twenty-five years; in fact, the editorial

Composition Studies 42.1 (2014): 123–127

description of *Composition Forum* from early print volumes is nearly identical to the language that appears on the journal's website today. Though the focus remains unchanged, the medium, methods of dissemination, genres, and topics of discussion have transformed in significant ways—largely a result of developments in digital publishing.

Like most journals in the early 2000s, *Composition Forum* faced challenges through rising publication costs, increasing diversity and rapid transformation of academic conversations, and the development of interest in hypertextual and multimodal alternatives to traditional print formats. Influenced in part by the CCCC's 1987 Position Statement on Scholarship in Composition, which recognized that the field embraces "many ways of presenting important new work in composition," volume 14.2 (Fall 2005) of *Composition Forum* transitioned from a print-based to a web-based format. The journal's decade-long transfiguration has attempted to balance the strengths of traditional methods of scholarly publication (primarily the long-form print-based essay) with new media possibilities for emergent multimodal genres and increased access to published materials.

Through this transition, we see three significant themes—three A's of digital publishing—that authors, editors, and readers should consider regarding digital publishing in rhetoric and composition journals: the evolution and development of *argumentation* styles, the role of *authority* in print versus electronic scholarship, and the ways in which *accessibility* can be affected by digital technologies.

Argumentation Styles

The editors saw various good reasons for moving from print to digital, though abandoning the long-form essay was not one of them. Rather, we wished to expand upon this genre to enable scholars to present their work in ways that best suited them. James Purdy and Joyce Walker suggest that we might reconsider the print-digital binary opposition by thinking less about "whether a text is visual or print and more about what it produces, participates in, or does" (191). We believe that the essay can be a useful vehicle for discussions and analysis of the intersections between composition theory and pedagogy, regardless of how and where it is published. Though it seems popular to disparage the essay, we still see its merits for disseminating scholarly work. It provides a useful avenue for a sustained and carefully developed argument; it enables scholars to draw upon source material and referential data; and as we address below, the essay is a familiar and widely accepted genre in academia. Consequently, we sought to expand our notions of the essay and other scholarly writing genres rather than abandoning them or radically transforming them in digital formats.

With that premise in mind, the styles, genres, and types of scholarship published in *Composition Forum* have steadily broadened in the journal's post-print volumes. Many of the articles published in the journal continue to rely upon the conventional long-form essay structure, though there has been a continued increase in multimedia components within those articles. Our book reviews have similarly accounted for the digital shift, offering reviews of online and multimodal texts, while also incorporating images, sounds, and direct links to the works themselves and to related digital material. The electronic format has also facilitated the inclusion of new genres, most notably the program profile and the retrospective essay. These two most recent additions to the journal reflect our growing awareness of writing as an ecology—an awareness that is influenced and reflected by digital media—since both the program profile and the retrospective essay seek to situate scholarship, teaching, and program development as well as prior texts in relation to the breadth of work in the field. In many ways, we've found the digital format to be a vehicle of freedom from the confines of the printed text, particularly in how it allows for the publication of diverse styles and approaches as well as the flexibility to make publication decisions solely on textual merit rather than space and page-length considerations. In short, the shift from print to digital has facilitated an expansion of the genres and types of scholarship published in *Composition Forum*, and we see this expansion continuing in the future.

Authority

An unfortunate quality of digital publishing is the continued skepticism of its legitimacy and rigor compared to traditional print-based scholarly publication. Over the past two decades there have been significant strides in pushing against such perceptions, with journals like *Kairos, Enculturation*, and *Computers and Composition Online* demonstrating the potential of multimodal electronic publication (see Ball and Moeller). *Composition Forum's* current format demonstrates that electronic texts that are simultaneously web- and print-friendly can offer much to the conversation on publication "value." Linear, text-based digital articles provide a familiar format for tenure and promotion committees at institutions where multimodal or otherwise nontraditional texts might be viewed with apprehension. At the same time, the digital format and emergent genres in the journal allow authors to express themselves in diverse ways, drawing upon multimodal approaches to supplement and enhance text.

Consequently, we envision *Composition Forum's* current structure as a means of satisfying the needs of traditional authors and reviewers while also accommodating new ways of creating and disseminating scholarly work. We recognize that this approach could be viewed as overly pragmatic, seeming to support a notion of linear text as the most (if not only) legitimate mode for academic scholarship. However, we believe that web texts with a more recognizable form or structure should be viewed as conceptually related both to traditional forms of publication and to nonlinear, multimodal, and other experiments in online composition. That is, linear web texts can serve as a kind of "low bridge" for electronic skeptics to recognize digital scholarship as valuable and as rigorously reviewed as print scholarship, even while the essay genre itself gets redefined through the broad shift toward composition for digital media. Similarly, this model may also encourage experimentation and evolution in the texts created by authors who are new to or wary of multimodal genres.

Accessibility

One of the greatest difficulties for print and electronic publication alike is the issue of *accessibility*, of inventing and increasing opportunities for similar engagement experiences with a given text by the widest variety of readers possible—especially when, as noted above, there might be resistance to a critical acceptance of electronic publication. While digital technologies have made it increasingly easy for authors to experiment and publish in numerous modes of communication, those same technologies are unfortunately not always accessible to varied populations of readers. The most accessible web format remains *text*, due to its ability to be interpreted by screen reader software (for visually impaired readers), its relatively small file size (for readers with limited download capabilities or slow access to the Internet), and its print-friendly capability.

Composition Forum remains dedicated to disseminating scholarly work to as broad an academic audience as possible—accessibility is a primary aim of the journal. Our dedication to accessibility includes complying with W3C standards and the goals of the Web Standards Project to make it possible for all readers to engage the same content, regardless of device, browser, or reading preference or constraint. Currently, the editors are redesigning the site to improve further the reading experience across browsers and media/devices (e.g., desktops, tablets, smartphones), including a technical upgrade to the responsiveness of the site and a structural shift from XHTML 1.0 to HTML 5. The open-access nature of the journal is also central to this goal; moving away from a paid subscription base expands access to a wider potential audience.

Conclusions

Composition Forum has supported digital publishing initiatives with a three-pronged approach focused on expanding argumentation styles in the genres we publish, extending the authority of print to digital scholarship, and increasing access to published content. As forms and methods of digital scholarship evolve further, our strategies will adapt and develop accordingly. While we do not foresee the long-form essay disappearing, we want to celebrate the critical value of emerging digital genres and give them equal footing with traditional scholarship. Though the shift from print to digital has been neither quick nor universal, we continue to value the merits of rigorous peer-review as the primary apparatus for maintaining the authority of scholarly material. We also envision further technological changes and the impacts they will have on digital publishing, and accessibility must remain at the forefront of innovation in digital publishing. Greater attention to these issues will only improve how the field composes and evaluates electronic publication.

Works Cited

Ball, Cheryl E., and Ryan Moeller. "Converging the ASS[umptions] Between U and ME; or How New Media Can Bridge a Scholarly/Creative Split in English Studies." *Computers and Composition Online* (2008): n. pag. Web. 25 Feb. 2014. <http://www2.bgsu.edu/departments/english/cconline/convergence/index.html>.

Conference on College Composition and Communication. (1987). "Scholarship in Composition: Guidelines for Faculty, Deans, and Department Chairs." CCCC Position Statement. Web. 20 Feb. 2014. <http://www.ncte.org/cccc/resources/positions/scholarshipincomp>.

"Editorial Policy." *Composition Forum*. Web. 25 Feb. 2014. <http://compositionforum.com/editorial-policy.php>.

Harter, Stephen P., and Hak Joon Kim. "Electronic Journals and Scholarly Communication: A Citation and Reference Study." *Information Research* 2.1 (1996): n. pag. Web. 25 Feb. 2014. <http://www.informationr.net/ir/2-1/paper9a.html>.

Purdy, James P., and Joyce R. Walker. "Valuing Digital Scholarship: Exploring the Changing Realities of Intellectual Work." *Profession* (2010): 177–95. Print.

Web Standards Project. *The Web Standards Project*. Web. 18 Feb. 2014. <http://www.webstandards.org/>.

Book Reviews

Hacking Composition: Rethinking Codeswitching in Writing Discourse

Language Mixing and Code-Switching in Writing: Approaches to Mixed-Language Written Discourse, edited by Mark Sebba, Shahrzad Mahootian, and Carla Jonsson. New York: Routledge, 2012. 280 pp.

Language and Mobility: Unexpected Places, by Alastair Pennycook. Toronto: Multilingual Matters, 2012. 189 pp.

Translingual Practice: Global Englishes and Cosmopolitan Relations, by Suresh Canagarajah. New York: Routledge, 2013. 216 pp.

Reviewed by Shakil Rabbi, Pennsylvania State University

In *True to the Language Game,* Keith Gilyard questions the efficacy of "code-switching pedagogy," stating that there are "no reputable studies demonstrating that speech varieties translate neatly into writing varieties, no possibility that teachers can teach appropriateness" (129). He concludes his criticisms with calls for a reevaluation of the term "code" in the context of its sociolinguistic origins. He also highlights a striking assumption by composition as a field: that we have prematurely adopted a pedagogy developed through research on spoken language varieties without assessing its applicability for written discourse. This questions the field's implicit marking of codeswitching[1] as unconventional and illegitimate. At best, writing teachers say codeswitching is acceptable in community exchanges but not in professional or high stakes settings.

What is needed is critical literature that studies codeswitching in written discourse as thoroughly as that which has been developed for the oral forms of the phenomenon. The three books reviewed in this essay advance exactly such a project. The first book, *Language Mixing and Code-Switching in Writing*, illustrates language mixing in written discourse historically and in our contemporary time. The subsequent works, *Language and Mobility* and *Translingual Practice,* generate useful frames to discuss codeswitching as rhetorical practices of contact zones that can inform our writing pedagogy. In developing these frames, the latter two books abandon the term codeswitching in favor of other labels for approaching this form of written practice.

* * *

Language Mixing and Code-Switching in Writing: Approaches to Mixed Language Written Discourse, edited by Mark Sebba, Shahrzad Mahootian, and Carla Jonsson, provides analyses of a variety of multilingual or codeswitched texts. In his introduction to the collection, Sebba argues that a monolingual bias in writing scholarship has resulted in an absence of an "independent, theoretically informed field of multilingual discourse studies" (2). This is a significant oversight for the field as Mahootian states in his chapter "Repertoires and Resources: Accounting for Code-Mixing in the Media": "[M]ultilingualism is a norm . . . [meaning that] human language capacity assumed to be present in the language acquisition device[s] applies equally across monolingual and multilingual contexts" (193).

The essays making up this collection show ways to start mapping this multilingual norm. They present analyses of multilingual texts utilizing methods such as corpus analysis (Schendl; Nurmi and Pahta; Montes-Alcalá; Sebba), ethnography and new literacy studies approaches (Kytölä; Lee and Barton; Vold Lexander; Mbodj-Pouye and Van den Avenne), and discourse analysis (Mahootian; Jonsson; Leppänen; Angermeyer). The chapters look at texts such as medieval letters (Schendl; Nurmi and Pahta) and sermons (Schendl), miscellaneous contemporary print texts (Mahootian; Sebba; Mbodj-Pouye and Van den Avenne), novels (Montes-Alcalá; Jonsson), digital texts (Kytölä; Lee and Barton; Vold Lexander; Leppänen), and visual texts (Angermeyer).

Two chapters in particular struck me as novel analyses of current codeswitching writing practices. The first, "Vernacular Literacy Practices in Present-day Mali: Combining Ethnography and Textual Analysis to Understand Texts," by Aissatou Mbodj-Pouye and Cécile Van den Avenne, looks at noninstitutional writing in spaces such as the personal notebooks of "low-literate writers" in the multilingual developing nation of Mali (which is one example of the type of contact zone Alastair Pennycook and Suresh Canagarajah deliberate on as well). The researchers find that the texts they analyze use multiple scripts and diagrams with skillful consistency—reiterating Gilyard's comment about the complex nature of codes—and show that codeswitching on paper exhibits a "fluidity in language and script choice, interferences between languages and a degree of code-mixing... [as well as] a sense of norms and genres" (170). Their focus on low-literate writers is also significant because most of the current scholarship on written codeswitching looks at texts produced in classrooms and overlooks the subjects and settings Mbodj-Pouye and Van den Avenne study here. Their findings—that though low-literate writers are not "fully equipped to align their practices to their language choices," they are still able "to deal with this situation in creative and unexpected ways" (170)—are reminiscent of important work on "basic writers" in composition studies (see Shaughnessy).

The second chapter that I want to highlight, "Linguistic and Generic Hybridity in Web Writing: The Case of Fan Fiction" by Sirpa Leppanen, views the space of the internet as the quintessential contact zone, simultaneously local and global. It is this recognition of the global orientation of digital media, Leppanen argues, that drives the young Finnish writers of the fan fiction texts he studies to develop multilingual repertoires made up of English and Finnish. He concludes that the forms of codeswitching in the 700 fan fiction texts he studied are heteroglossia, "motivated by the translocality of the webspace," and characterized by writing practices that are "fundamentally indexical activities, allowing participants to come together as communities of practice with their shared cultures and orders of normativity" (250). This is a critically important explanation of the effect of the digital medium: Leppanen points out that the internet provides a potential third space for new modes of articulation (where multilingualism is the dominant norm), but also argues that this space reproduces the indexical priority of English as an imperial language on a new translocal scale. Taken together, these two chapters remind us that the medium of written codeswitching (paper notebooks, the internet, writing itself, etc.) is important to understand the message and that written codeswitching fundamentally differs from oral varieties. As a whole, the collection is valuable to the field for its expansion of studies of written multilingualism, extending into texts not ordinarily examined in composition studies. However, as it stops short of attempting to theorize such phenomena, the book's findings and effects on pedagogy are fleshed out only when read in conjunction with books such as Pennycook's and Canagarajah's.

* * *

If *Language Mixing and Code-Switching in Writing* is to be read in terms of a descriptive treatment of codeswitching, Pennycook's *Language and Mobility: Unexpected Places* argues for reading certain codeswitching texts as everyday, unprivileged practices of the contact zone. In other words, Pennycook's treatment is critical. Specifically targeting colonial and modern globalized spaces, he writes that texts of the contact zone are productively approached as "an emotional and temporal journey" and "an exploration of mnemonic traces, of those sensual and tactile pieces of history that connect across unexpected places" (173). The point, for Pennycook, is to look at how the historical context enables a multimodal reading of monolingualism. Chapter one is written like a travelogue, overlaying his journey to South India with details from his grandparents' migrations during the British Empire era. Pennycook conceptualizes codeswitching as emerging out of mobility and mnemonic traces and as functioning as an index of affective experiences. Chapters two and three build on this conceptualization, extending it to discussions on sports, language, and pedagogy as social practices. It is a way for him to effect a "critical resistance" in language research, a way to push against the norms of academic epistemology, and to foreground what Michel Foucault calls *penser autrement* (thinking otherwise) through "accounts that interweave family history, travel, language and culture" (17).

Chapters four and six will interest writing scholars and theorists of globalization directly. First, by analyzing a series of letters by his grandparents in chapter four, Pennycook presents what he terms epistolary parenting. He explains that these letters were the primary form of interactions between colonial subjects and families separated by thousands of miles; the letters were communicative tracts that "needed to do so much, to connect, to nurture, to advise, to admonish, to encourage, to direct" (72). In this way, he explains, epistolary parenting functioned to keep families together across the distances of the British Empire and as such can shed light on how "patterns of communication continue under [current] conditions of global communication" (72). Second, the letters evidence how "Indian words, or their Anglo-Indian variants, crept into unexpected places in the language and letters of these colonial workers" (57). While Anglo-Indians are not the focus of linguistic paradigms such as World Englishes, these letters illustrate a need to see English hybridization as something used by socially privileged groups, as well as the peripheral subjects often termed *non-native English speakers*. These findings by Pennycook present significant parallels to the multilingual correspondences of aristocratic English women in the early modern period, analyzed in the chapter by Arja Nurmi and Päivi Pahta in *Language Mixing and Code-Switching in Writing*: both exhibit a multilingual literacy by women and a concern with everyday practices in the private sphere of women and the family.

Chapter six looks at a series of written farewell addresses gifted as souvenirs to Anglo-Indian managers by the colonial staff, and an open letter to the Dewan, or chief minister, of Travencore. These texts evidence writing that "locates [such farewell utterances] within (Southern) Indian forms of address and interaction, while also acknowledging the overlay of English and colonial relations" (115). Pennycook's analyses of the texts admirably avoid the pitfalls of "invoking an 'Indian style' of writing," and successfully articulate them as "*mnemonic traces* [sic] . . . of caste, of other languages, of other rhetorical styles[,] . . . of how Indian officials and European managers occupied parallel positions in India at the time . . . [and of] how a certain genre can develop" (116-17). This is Pennycook at his best and is the most consequential part of the book. First, his evocative analysis presents an opportunity to reinterpret the dated arguments of contrastive rhetoric by framing these letters as writing practices that layer various codes in a manner that Mary Louise Pratt has called "transculturation," or the selective borrowing of dominant cultural forms by a subordinated culture for the purposes of accessing power and resisting domination (6). It is a contribution that adds to the current debate in composition studies on English usage in contact zones and which Canagarajah also comments on in his treatment of codemeshing in his book and in his 2006 article, "The Place of World Englishes in Composition: Pluralization Continued." Second, Pennycook says that a study of such texts has much to say about understanding our contemporary global society, where fast-food workers and call center workers in developing nations such as India and the Philippines are required to learn the idioms of American English and therefore "may be part of the same linguistically regulated class formation," yet have "material class positions [that] may vary quite considerably" (123).

Chapters five and seven weigh in on the long debate over the binary of the native speaker (NS)–nonnative speaker (NNS) category by articulating a critical commentary on the binary of the pedagogy theorist and the practicing teacher. Pennycook says that seeing languages as local practice (his previous book is *Language as a Local Practice*) reorients language pedagogies according to a "local understanding of [the] social operation of language and power," and "locate[s] the capacity to speak in the social domain" (87). However, these two chapters represent the weakest sections in the book. His method of outlining "at least thirteen ways of looking at a blackboard" does not reach a substantial conclusion (Canagarajah proposes the notion of performative competence to address a similar issue) nor does it inform the practical ways in which power differentials and gaps between academics and practicing teachers might be reconfigured.

The final chapter turns to the mobility and transformation of social practices on a global scale by looking at the example of cricket. Here Pennycook presents a stimulating recapitulation of the classic postcolonial reading of the history of the sport by C. L. R. James, Ashis Nandy, and Arjun Appadurai. He frames India as the irrefutable center of modern cricket, a fact he says can teach us a great deal about the future of English and the teaching of English.[2] This chapter reads like a work out of cultural studies and reiterates Pennycook's basic argument that "we are not in fact 'native speakers' of things called 'languages' so much as we engage in local language practices . . . becoming a *resourceful speaker* is what we are surely aiming at, an idea that embraces both the ability to accommodate others and to manipulate different resources" (172). This chapter responds to Gilyard's call to reexamine the status of "code" in codeswitching, though in the form of speculative theorizing of language and its traces as an historical phenomenon.

* * *

Translingual Practice: Global Englishes and Cosmopolitan Practices will interest anyone involved in language use and language teaching. Whereas the previous two works look at codeswitching texts in terms of social practices, this book presents a critical deliberation of potential meaning for the language classroom. Building on recent conversations around translingualism in composition by prominent scholars such as Bruce Horner, John Trimbur, Min-Zhan Lu, and Jacqueline Jones Royster, among others, Canagarajah proposes a new episteme that extends notions of multilingualism, one where "communication transcends individual languages [and] transcends words and involves diverse semiotic resources and ecological affordances" (6). Translingualism, as a theoretical approach, is an ambitious one, and given the scope of *Translingual Practice*, addresses a multiplicity of fields, such as rhetoric and composition, writing studies, applied linguistics, sociolinguistics, and globalization studies.

Canagarajah begins the book by recounting the composing process of a student in his class who *codemeshed*—his preferred term, as he finds that codeswitching in writing pedagogy still segregates and hierarchizes linguistic codes. In chapter two, translingualism is presented as denying the problematic notion of unified languages articulated by models based on the Herderian-triad, "the equivalence of language, community and place," and redefining linguistic systems as dynamic structures perpetually in flux (20). Canagarajah presents monolingualism as a false hegemonic construction of modernism, which denies, among other things, how Westerners themselves actually used language before the advent of various national projects in the West. The medieval texts—sermons and tracts—studied by Schendl in his essay in *Language Mixing and Code-Switching in Writing* directly support this latter point by illustrating forms of functional multilingualism based on audience awareness.

Chapters three, four, and five argue for the historical continuity and universality of translanguaging and posit what translingualism means in language scholarship. First, using pre-colonial, pre-modern examples from South Asia and beyond, Canagarajah writes, "translingual practices may not be as difficult or esoteric as we might assume... It is monolingual communication that might seem strange to many" (55). Second, translingualism is presented as an expansion of World Englishes, English as an International Language, and English as Lingua Franca models, and is thereby informed by decades of scholarship. However, what sets translingualism apart from these other approaches is its focus on English as the incorporation of non-linguistic elements in communication, enabling a way of understanding "how unshared words or grammatical structures gain situated meaning" by attending to "the local contexts and practices of negotiation with the fullest ecological resources" (75). Despite efforts by scholars in these schools to address the diversity of

English, their arguments still assume a need for shared norms because their models assume them.

In terms of what codeswitching means vis-à-vie translingualism, Canagarajah's illustration of it in chapter five through the formulation of a "grammar of practices" is as clear a presentation one is going to get of such a speculative concept. Analyzing interactions between a group of students—made up of native and nonnative speakers, subjects of European and non-European descent—at a UK university, he provides a close analysis of the strategies of "envoicing, recontextualization, interactional, and entextualization" and explains how language scholars might use these concepts to understand communicative interactions in the contact zone of the university (77-79). Chapters six and seven build on this "grammar of practice" to see how it holds up as a way to understand standard written English, particularly in academic contexts, and how negotiations making up the composition processes might be analyzed to identify generative meaning. Skillfully using examples to develop a comparison between the codemeshing strategies used in a 1999 article by respected scholar Geneva Smitherman and the student-text he presents in his introduction, Canagarajah explains how writers might effectively deploy "recontextualization and entextualization… [to] agentively develop new meanings and values for [their] codes as [they] pluralize dominant norms and literacies" (126). Canagarajah also writes that in order to understand codemeshing texts we need new literate practices and reciprocal reading strategies, which are best learned with experience. Gilyard's point about teachers not being able to teach appropriateness vis-à-vis codeswitching seems particularly pertinent here. Teachers need to understand contextually the effectiveness of such practices and their instructional potential, particularly given the impossibility of reproducing the conditions such moves require in environments like the classroom.

Chapters eight and nine take on the notion of agency and how it functions in the face of the normative discourses of standardized English and grammar. Citing a series of interviews with skilled migrants in the UK, Canagarajah makes the case that non-native speakers of English are not overwhelmingly the victims of normative discourses—an argument that seemingly replies to Jan Blommaert's writings on language mobility and global scales in *The Sociolinguistics of Globalization*. Rather, the responses by these skilled migrants show virtual spaces that are "polyaccented, multilingual, and plural," constructing a translingual space and scale that deviates from the power of "standard English" (163). By creating and utilizing these spaces, Canagarajah says migrants become agents who "contest [the imposition of center-norms] in their own negotiation strategies" and "redefine the translocal space to their advantage" (170).

To understand the negotiation strategies of a translingual approach, Canagarajah proposes what he terms *performative competence*, as opposed to grammatical competence (of monolingualism) or communicative competence (of multilingualism). In a fitting response to the exigence that Pennycook raises about the disconnect between theorist-pedagogues and practicing teachers, Canagarajah defines performative competence as a concept more adept at addressing the interactions in classrooms because it explicitly accounts for the "dynamic and reciprocal strategies" used by interlocutors (174). A translingual approach assumes that meanings in the classroom emerge through dialogic practices, and so performative competence facilitates pedagogy with ways to "find the right balance between writers' voices and readers' uptakes . . . all leading to the appropriate sense of coherence, meaning and rhetorical effectiveness" (188).

The final chapter connects these discussions on translingual practices and the ideology derived from them to current philosophical and normative deliberations on cosmopolitanism. Canagarajah appropriates Anthony Appiah's metaphor of conversations to present his understanding of emergent cosmopolitan subjectivity, arguing that conversations are the universal practice through which all individuals understand each other. He sees an emphasis on the dialogism of intercultural conversation as providing insights into cosmopolitanism's theoretical impasse. Dialogic cosmopolitanism, as articulated through translingualism, affirms the identities of communities based on historical investments while also explaining how they might engage with other communities to develop new coconstructed identities and values.

* * *

The three books reviewed here approach codeswitching as rhetorical practices of contact zones and analyze how they function as communication and articulation. In response to Gilyard's call to rethink the term *code*, all three works reinterpret linguistic codes as symbolic practices of "so many linguistic habitus which are at least partially orchestrated, and of the oral production of these habitus" (Bourdieu 46). Read in the context of the descriptions of multilingualism-as-norm addressed in the collection by Sebba, Mahootian, and Jonsson, both Pennycook's and Canagarajah's books can be seen as appropriately advocating for teaching strategically to contest power differentials between languages and as part of a poststructuralist critical project. Pennycook shows that contemporary English language and global society carry traces of historical mixing and no one approach or view of language pedagogy can account for all varieties. Canagarajah's call for a translingual approach posits an entirely new episteme and pedagogy of language-study in terms of its semiotic ecology rather than distinct linguistic systems. Read together, these books articulate a critical point: assuming multilingualism as the norm fundamentally transforms how we have to think of the field of composition studies. A lot more needs to be done in this area, but these three books are a good beginning.

We also have to remember that rhetorical theory teaches that audience is critical to understanding how languages are used. The three books under review only nominally deliberate on the role of the reader in written codeswitching, a gap that needs to be filled. Future scholarship has to account for the question of reception, or how codeswitched texts are read and the ethics of such readings. Skillful writing encodes multiple layers of information and rhetorical appeals into texts to facilitate the communication and interpretation of such works. Audiences, for their part, grant authority to the writer before they even engage with the logic of an utterance. "Indeed," Gilyard reminds us, "writing is largely an exercise in creating the listener" (119). However, the take on written codeswitching as rhetorical practices by these books does foreground a holistic approach to writing that includes both the production and reception aspect of texts, and thereby asks the kinds of questions which will inevitably lead to greater scholarly, pedagogical, and theoretical development of the field.

State College, Pennsylvania

Notes

1. I follow the conventions of prominent sociolinguistic journals such as *Language in Society* and *Journal in Sociolinguistics* in using *codeswitching* as a de-hyphenated term.

2. India has the largest self-identified English speaking population in the world and most of them use multiple languages simultaneously as normal linguistic practice.

Works Cited

Blommaert, Jan. *The Sociolinguistics of Globalization.* Cambridge: Cambridge UP, 2010. Print.

Bourdieu, Pierre. *Language and Symbolic Power.* Trans. Gino Raymond and Matthew Adamson. Cambridge: Harvard UP, 1991. Print.

Canagarajah, Suresh. "The Place of World Englishes in Composition: Pluralization Continued." *College Composition and Communication* 57.4 (2006): 586-619. Print.

Gilyard, Keith. *True to the Language Game: African American Discourse, Cultural Politics, and Pedagogy.* New York: Routledge, 2011. Print.

Pennycook, Alastair. *Language as a Local Practice.* New York: Routledge, 2010. Print.

Pratt, Mary Louise. *Imperial Eyes: Travel Writing and Transculturation.* New York: Routledge, 1992. Print.

Shaughnessey, Mina. *Errors and Expectations: A Guide for the Teacher of Basic Writing.* New York: Oxford UP, 1997. Print.

Understanding the Impacts of Participatory, Digital Technologies on Classroom Practices

Participatory Composition: Video Culture, Writing, and Electracy, by Sarah J. Arroyo. Carbondale: SIUP, 2013. 169 pp.

Teaching Literature and Language Online, edited by Ian Lancashire. New York: MLA, 2009. 440 pp.

Reviewed by Carl Whithaus, University of California, Davis

Participatory Composition, by Sarah J. Arroyo, and *Teaching Literature and Language Online*, edited by Ian Lancashire, take up a central question for college humanities faculty: how do we incorporate emerging forms of technology in language, writing, and literature courses? In response, Arroyo's book explores the collaborative culture developing around YouTube videos. Informed by Gregory Ulmer's writing on "electracy," Arroyo creates a framework for understanding the participatory dynamics around video sharing and social media; she also examines the implications of this participatory rhetoric for the teaching of writing. Lancashire's *Teaching Literature and Language Online* does not focus on video but rather casts a wider net as the contributors explore how information technologies are reshaping pedagogy and learning in writing, language, and literature courses. In his introduction, Lancashire argues that "there are three key perspectives on online teaching: the institution's, the teacher's, and the student's" (1). The organization of *Teaching Literature and Language Online*, however, does not directly mirror these three perspectives. Instead, it is divided into three parts that examine (1) the range of approaches to online education across different MLA disciplines, (2) case studies of online language courses, and (3) case studies of online literature courses. Many of the chapters take into account institutional issues, faculty perspectives, and, to a lesser degree, student views. At first, the objectives and organizational structures of these two books may appear disparate from each other, but there is a synergy that emerges as they are read together.

Both works try to formulate pedagogical responses to the increasingly participatory digital technologies that are reshaping the ways public and educational discourses operate. Arroyo's work explores the implications of YouTube and video sharing for composition studies; Lancashire's wide-ranging, multi-authored collection about teaching languages, writing, and literature online addresses an evolution within not only humanities research but also within humanities teaching. It should be noted that Lancashire's book is the older of the two. It was published in 2009, while *Participatory Composition* just came out in 2013. In addition, many of the chapters in *Teaching Literature and Language Online* discuss online courses or course materials used during the mid 2000s. The datedness of the pieces in *Teaching Literature and Language Online* somewhat limits our ability to draw immediate, practical lessons from them for our own classrooms in 2014. Also, the disjuncture between the work's 2009 publication date and the time when the online courses and materials were developed speaks to the problem of timeliness in terms of humanities scholarship, especially humanities scholarship about teaching—it's too slow. Jerome McGann takes this problem as his starting point in "Humane Studies in Digital Space," one of six essays in part one of *Teaching Literature and Language Online.* McGann argues that to counter this problem of the slow availability of humanities publications "educators and scholars need professionally sanctioned online-publishing mechanisms" (90). It is an interesting claim about the need for officially recognized research and teaching materials, one that runs in a different direction from much of what Arroyo develops in *Participatory Composition.* That is, while McGann is focused on scholars' production of critical materials and their dissemination to students, Arroyo is interested in students' production of their own digital compositions. Arroyo's book is about a rhetorical education where the students themselves are participating in and creating online cultural spaces.

Still, reading *Participatory Composition* and *Teaching Literature and Language Online* together encouraged me to think beyond the divide between writing studies and literary studies. These texts also encouraged me to think about the ways in which college faculty who teach courses on languages, writing, or literature wrestle with similar issues as we reshape our teaching in face-to-face, hybrid, and online courses and take advantage of digital technologies in order to increase opportunities for student participation. Humanities faculty who work in languages, writing, and literature are adapting pedagogies to work with the multimodal forms of discourse that students are increasingly encountering within their academic, social, and professional lives. Working to develop those pedagogies is challenging, but Arroyo's and Lancashire's books make the task easier by theorizing and providing specific classroom examples that showcase how methods of teaching languages, writing, and literature shift in promising directions in our digital age.

Arroyo's *Participatory Composition* engages with Gregory Ulmer's concept of "electracy" and the work of "Florida School" writers such as Jeff Rice, Craig Saper, Michael Jarrett, Barry Mauer, and Marcel O'Gorman (see Rice and O'Gorman). While Arroyo's introduction is careful to situate her project in relation to previous work on "electracy," as a whole the book extends well beyond advocating for an updated approach to the personalized, digital narratives that Ulmer advocated having students write as "MyStories." Chapter two, "Recasting Subjectivity for Electracy," documents the collaborative culture developing around YouTube videos. Arroyo engages and challenges critiques of YouTube use within higher education put forward by Henry Jenkins and Alexandra Juhasz. Particularly interesting is Arroyo's response to Juhasz's view of YouTube as being fundamentally organized around popularity and driven by the frivolous (42-45). Arroyo contends that "while popularity is certainly an organizing structure on YouTube, it doesn't serve as the only catalyst that brings people to the site" (43). For Arroyo, YouTube videos can be innovative within higher education classes because the medium does not replicate the forms of discourse or writing used in textual or live, face-to-face interactions. In addition to the medium of video shifting rhetorical delivery and reception, YouTube is a social media platform. Its logic and practices do not break neatly into professional/amateur or commercial/community dichotomies. Instead, Arroyo argues, YouTube is an emerging set of creative, rhetorical, and social practices that facilitate a continuum of cultural productions and participatory actions. Higher education classes—particularly those focused on rhetoric and composition—should engage students directly not only in thinking about YouTube as a participatory space but also in having students participate in the rhetorical contexts opened up by online video sharing and social media platforms.

It is at this moment in her book that Arroyo begins to go beyond Ulmer and other "Florida School" writers' previous work. Chapter three, "The Question of Definition," returns to the ancient rhetorical concepts of *stasis* and *chora*. Arroyo blends Ulmer's take on *chora* with Victor Vitanza's work on countertheses and Collin Brooke's concept of *proairesis*. Citing Vitanza's *Negation, Subjectivity, and the History of Rhetoric*, Arroyo considers the implications of rhetorical and social systems creating boundaries between the included and the excluded. She takes Vitanza's insight that "Wherever there is a system (totality, unity), there is the trace of the excluded" (4) and argues that it is "one of the most provocative yet pressing notions for our discussion: asking what something is, in order to define and set up boundaries, undoubtedly excludes and purges that which it is not" (Arroyo 51). By tracing the historical significance within rhetoric and composition studies of *stasis* theory as a method of limiting the scope of an argument and as a means of developing topoi appropriate to that argument (49-54), Arroyo sets up a response that recuperates *chora*, the movement or flow of an argument, rather than focusing on how to limit an argument as a vital step in the invention and composition process. Brooke's concept of *proairesis*, as well as the participatory practices of "tubing" and sharing that exist in the rhetorical space of YouTube, informs Arroyo's work at this point. I cannot hope to do justice to Arroyo's subtle argument in my limited space here, but her valuing of *chora* as part of rhetorical invention is beautifully illustrated—unsurprisingly—in "The Dancing Floor," a work available as both a YouTube video (Alaei and Arroyo) and as a scholarly article in *Kairos* (Arroyo and Alaei).

While Jenkins, Juhasz, and others have dismissed YouTube based on a logic of frivolous popularity, and while rhetorical theory has valued *stasis* and *topoi* as means of facilitating invention for student writers, Arroyo offers us an alternative—choric processes for invention that value the sharing and participatory cultural practices students may already be familiar with from sites such as YouTube. What is significant about her work is that it not only extends Ulmer's "electracy" to account for YouTube and other Web 2.0 technologies but that Arroyo also links cultural theory to implications for pedagogical practices. Her penultimate chapter, "Participatory Pedagogy: Merging Postprocess and Postpedagogy," is essential reading for composition studies scholars. Arroyo traces the interplay among theory and practice in digital spaces where shifts in writing technologies never slow down enough to allow mastery in the old sense of the term. She argues for a composition praxis that embraces online videos and collaboration, but it is not those forms or media alone that Arroyo urges us to value. Instead, it is the participatory, the action of teaching and learning as dialogue among students and teachers, among participants, that she would have us value.

Aligning Thomas Kent's work on postprocess theory and Vitanza's advocacy for postpedagogy, Arroyo reminds us that her project is not primarily about sharing online videos, rather it is about developing participatory practices in higher education courses focused on writing and rhetoric. She urges writing teachers to blend rhetorical theories and pedagogical practices "[b]y both working with established forms as well as inventing new ones as they become timely and necessary. This act requires letting go of the idea that when we teach writing in all of its manifestations, we are transmitting a body of knowledge based on a solid theoretical foundation" (111). *Participatory Composition* is a challenge to business as usual in college writing and rhetoric courses. That challenge may at first seem to be about YouTube—videos as possible compositions in writing courses—but if read carefully, Arroyo's book reaches well beyond debates about how many multimodal assignments to include in a first-year composition course. *Participatory Composition* asks us to think not about *how* we value the writing students create and that we grade, but rather about *what* we want to value in the process of learning.

In reaching out to these larger questions regarding what to value when learning about languages, writing, and literature, Lancashire's collection does not begin with a focus on online videos. Instead he creates a wider arena in which he outlines how emerging forms of information technology impact the contributors' pedagogy and learning in writing, language, and literature courses. With its focus on online learning in the humanities, *Teaching Literature and Language Online* brings together essays from what would feel like disparate research communities in other circumstances. Where else would an overview section include essays from a noted scholar of Spanish and linguistics (Robert Blake), an exemplary composition studies researcher (Kris Blair), and a renowned literary critic whose publications include critical digital editions of Dante Gabriel Rossetti's works (Jerome McGann)? *Teaching Literature and Language Online* encourages us to think about the ways in which available multimodal writing technologies are reshaping college classes. Like Arroyo, each of the contributors is concerned with how students are deeply immersed in working with texts and languages to foster understanding of their own—and others'—languages and cultures.

The exact challenges of reshaping college humanities courses to incorporate more digital technologies and to foster greater student participation vary across disciplines and languages. For instance, the challenges and already available source materials are markedly different for Murray McGillivray's work with students on Old English literary texts and Gillian Lord's efforts to use online tools to bring Aymara—a living indigenous language with approximately three million speakers in Bolivia, Peru, and Chile—to a wider audience "for educational purposes as well as to ensure the preservation of this stimulating language" (178). Lancashire's *Teaching Literature and Language Online* presents these different challenges by first outlining approaches to online courses from different disciplines represented in the Modern Language Association (MLA). The second section of the book presents case studies, such as Lord's discussion of developing online tools for teaching Aymara, focused on language learning. Part three digs into courses focused on helping students understand literary texts, such as the Shakespeare courses where Michael Best uses print, electronic, and multimedia technologies "to provide much more detail about the processes of teaching than [his] classroom courses usually do" (257), and James Fitzmaurice's use of WebCT discussion board posts to foster student writing that was more thoughtful and drew on more textual evidence than that produced "by reading content modules, or lectures" (269). Of course, some of the works in the last section, such as the already referenced chapter by McGillivray on developing an online course on Old English, include discussions of language learning as well as analysis of literary texts. Taken together the three parts of *Teaching Literature and Language Online* speak to the challenge of using digital technologies to foster student engagement with language learning and literary analysis activities.

On one level, these essays are less explicitly engaged with developing participatory classroom practices than Arroyo's work is. However, on another level, most of the essays in *Teaching Literature and Language Online* address how student engagement and participation become increasingly apparent—and vital for a course's success—when courses move into online venues. Kris Blair's "Writing as Process and Online Education" and Mary Ann Lyman-Hager's "Teaching World Languages Online" take up the issues of increasing student engagement and participation explicitly. Exploring their essays in slightly more depth offers us a chance to foray into the considerations around increasing student participation that play out in many of the contributions to *Teaching Literature and Language Online*.

Blair's piece is situated in relationship with Cindy Selfe's work on the importance of paying attention to writing technologies, Arthur W. Chickering and Zelda Gamson's "Seven Principles" for effective undergraduate education, and Lee Shulman's concept of "signature pedagogies" as important workshop learning styles in disciplines ranging from law to medicine to composition. Blair argues that "community formation involves more than the mere use of a discussion board or chat room; it requires significant planning and communication of learning outcomes to the students, as well as the documentation of faculty expectations of students to meet those outcomes" (42). At first, Blair's vision of a dynamic online writing course that centers on clearly communicating course outcomes may appear less robust, less rhizomatic, less student-centered than Arroyo's YouTube-based participatory composition; however, Blair is in many ways creating a space for the type of (re)thinking about learning in the digital age that Arroyo develops. Blair acknowledges that faculty are more likely to be digital immigrants than students. She suggests that both faculty and students need to be open to incorporating rapidly changing tools for writing in digital spaces. Her vision is one where administrators support faculty and students by providing time and managing workload expectations so that online writing courses can incorporate "the podcast, the blog, the wiki, or numerous other open-source tools" (47). Blair's chapter—like many of the chapters in *Teaching Literature and Language Online*—is both a call for help and a challenge to mid- and upper-level university administrators. It is possible to build online environments that foster participatory educational practices in writing, language, and literature courses, but, Blair reminds us, the potential success of these environments is limited by constraints that may be outside of the control of classroom teachers or even writing program administrators. Despite those limitations, the possibilities of using online tools to make courses more engaging and more memorable for students drives Blair and the other contributors of *Teaching Literature and Language Online* to articulate a vision of pedagogies and learning environments that may be as interactive and participatory as the ones advocated by Arroyo in *Participatory Composition*.

When approaching the concept of student participation in class, it would be typical for a composition studies expert to frame the debate as an opposition between approaches to teaching writing and approaches to teaching literature. That move would be a very English department centered way of considering pedagogical approaches. One of the valuable aspects of *Teaching Literature and Language Online* is its inclusion of diverse disciplines within the MLA. That is, this volume is not dedicated to the teaching of English (writing and literature) online, but to teaching the humanities online more broadly. If we wanted to sketch out the most recent and exciting work in participatory pedagogy, we could do worse than draw a Vin diagram that showed the overlap of language, literature, and writing pedagogies. Discussions of online education and digital humanities teaching may be a vehicle for bringing together faculty concerned about student learning and how the environments in which we work foster that learning through student participation.

The focus of Lyman-Hager's essay—as well as the pieces by Robert Blake, Dawn Formo and Kimberly Robinson Neary, Nike Arnold, Gillian Lord, and Douglas Morgenstern—suggests that participation in digital learning spaces is vital to conversations about pedagogies and student participation in courses. Lyman-Hager argues that "the task before language educators is to determine not whether online education (e-learning) functions less well, as well, or better than face-to-face learning but how to create face-to-face educational settings, blended online environments, and distance courses that . . . make participation in language communities memorable for students and relevant to their needs" (70). Her essay goes on to trace the development of pedagogical theories for language learning and teaching and to suggest the importance of moving beyond communicative competence. Drawing on the work of Renate A. Schulz and Claire Kramsch, Lyman-Hager uses theories of language learning to show that a language community's engagement with the full-range of semiotic practices creates a much richer learning experience than does an emphasis on comprehensive language (70-73). That is, motivation, interaction, and meaning are key elements to learning and using a language. Lyman-Hager's chapter draws parallels between the changes in (foreign) language pedagogies and developments in composition pedagogies in the last twenty-five years. For me, reading Lyman-Hager's essay suggests the need for richer dialogues among writing teachers and foreign language instructors. These conversations about writing—in and beyond writing in English—have already begun in pushes towards translingual approaches to composition studies (see Horner et al.) and in efforts to map how writing programs are administered around the global (see Thaiss et al). We may be at a point in composition studies—really in the humanities more generally—where student participation becomes a key term for designing pedagogical approaches and learning environments.

Both *Participatory Composition* and *Teaching Literature and Language Online* remind us that forms of language, writing, and literature are shifting, and that college humanities classes are increasingly incorporating digital elements. Arroyo's and Lancashire's books are important tools for rethinking how students and faculty learn together in our digital age. Participatory culture for Arroyo emerges from blending the rhetorical theories of Ulmer and Vitanza with the culture of "tubing"—the sharing culture of YouTube. In a similar manner, Lancashire's collection brings together disparate sources: researchers and teachers working in English, foreign languages, and composition studies. The commonalities among the essays in Lancashire's collection—their wrestling with how to increase student interaction and learning in online courses—are amplified when we consider them in relationship with Arroyo's call for developing a participatory culture within postsecondary educational environments. At first this call for increased participation may seem primarily focused on engaging students by having them write in formats that are multimodal (e.g., YouTube) and having them share those works in ways that are informed by preexisting social media models. And that is part of it. But a review of Arroyo's and Lancashire's books together drives me toward a larger conclusion, a larger challenge: how do we foster participatory environments where students may learn about writing across multiple modes, languages, and disciplines?

Composition studies has important perspectives to contribute to these conversations. The terrific work coming out of computers and composition—and I would include Arroyo's book in this category—needs to be read and considered by faculty teaching language and literature courses as well as by writing researchers. At the same time, Lancashire's book reminds me that those of us who have found our home in composition studies may need to look beyond the borders of our disciplinary home to consider how the affordances of digital texts open up multilingual and multidisciplinary spaces for student learning. Composition studies and our allied, or sub-, fields of professional writing, rhetoric, technical communication, and WAC/WID have been leaders in considering how digital texts offer more opportunities for multimodal forms of writing and teaching. If we move forward with more explicit discussions of writing as multilingual and multidisciplinary, we may find benefits not only for our students but also for ourselves.

Davis, California

Works Cited

Alaei, Bahareh, and Sarah J. Arroyo. "The Dancing Floor." MLA Annual Convention. Seattle. Jan. 2012. YouTube. https://www.youtube.com/watch?v=Q5e0-wR0Sh4. Web. 19 Jan. 2014.

Arroyo, Sarah J., and Bahareh Alaei "The Dancing Floor." "MoMLA: From Gallery to Webtext." *Kairos* 17.2 (2013): n. pag. Web. 19 Jan. 2014.

Brooke, Collin G. *Lingua Fracta: Toward a Rhetoric of New Media*. Cresskill, N.J: Hampton Press, 2009. Print.

Chickering, Arthur W., and Zelda F. Gamson, eds. *Applying the Seven Principles for Good Practice in Undergraduate Education*. San Francisco: Jossey-Bass, 1991. Print.

Horner, Bruce, Min-Zhan Lu, Jacqueline Jones Royster, and John Trimbur. "Language Difference in Writing: Toward a Translingual Approach." *College English* 73.3 (2011): 303-21. Print.

Jenkins, Henry. *Convergence Culture: Where Old and New Media Collide*. New York: New York UP, 2006. Print.

Juhasz, Alexandra. Learning from Youtube. Boston: MIT Press, 2010. http://vectors. usc.edu/projects/learningfromyoutube/. Web. 17 March 2014.

Kent, Thomas, ed. *Post-Process Theory: Beyond the Writing-Process Paradigm*. Carbondale: SIUP, 1999. Print.

Kramsch, Claire. "From Communicative Competence to Symbolic Competence." *Modern Language Journal* 90.2 (2006): 249-52. Print.

Kramsch, Claire, and Steven L. Thorn. "Foreign Language Learning as Global Communicative Practice." *Globalization and Language Teaching*. Ed. Deborah Cameron and David Block. New York: Routledge, 2002. 83-100. Print.

Rice, Jeff, and Marcel O'Gorman, eds. *New Media/New Methods: The Academic Turn from Literacy to Electracy*. Anderson, SC: Parlor P, 2008.

Schulz, Renate A. "Reevaluating Communicative Competence as a Major Goal in Postsecondary Language Requirement Courses." *Modern Language Journal* 90.2 (2006): 252-55. Print.

Selfe, Cynthia L. *Technology and Literacy in the Twenty-First Century: The Importance of Paying Attention*. Carbondale: SIUP, 1999. Print.

Shulman, Lee. "Pedagogies of Uncertainty." *Liberal Education* 91.2 (2005): n.pag. Web. 14 Jan. 2014.

Thaiss, Chris, Gerd Bräuer, Paula Carlino, Lisa Ganobcsik-Williams, and Aparna Sinha, eds. *Writing Programs Worldwide: Profiles of Academic Writing in Many Places*. Fort Collins, CO: WAC Clearinghouse, 2012. Web. 14 Jan. 2014.

Ulmer, Gregory L. *Teletheory: Grammatology in the Age of Video*. New York: Routledge, 1989. Print.

Vitanza, Victor J. *Negation, Subjectivity, and the History of Rhetoric*. Albany: SUNY P, 1997. Print.

21 Genres and How to Write Them, by Brock Dethier.
Logan: Utah State UP, 2013. 280 pp.

Reviewed by Gretchen L. Dietz, Miami University

21 Genres and How to Write Them is a textbook that aims to guide composition students in analyzing and adapting their writing to various genres. This work emerges out of process traditions in composition theory but explicitly takes genre as the central focus. Dethier worked with Don Murray at The University of New Hampshire for nineteen years and voices that his work is greatly indebted to Murray's thinking. At the same time, this textbook complicates and advances questions of a writer's process by paying specific attention to genres and genre analysis.

In the introduction, Dethier describes a genre as "a type, form, or category" and explains that "[w]e use familiar genres like 'lab report' and 'personal essay' without thinking about what rules and conventions govern the genre" (3). But while genres work because of rules and conventions, Dethier is also careful to note that the idea of genre is changing. In the past, genres were seen as static, but recent theorists have argued that genres are fluid. When writers stretch the conventions of genres, genres themselves evolve. Dethier also points out that "almost all texts mix genres" (3). For example, because a simple two paragraph letter can contain description, narration, analysis, persuasion, and summary, "[t]he question is not whether you're going to integrate different genres but how you're going to integrate them" (3). This textbook stresses practicing different "moves" a writer can make. Dethier cautions that genres will change, but the moves a writer employs can work across different genres of writing (4).

21 Genres is designed as a reference and although Dethier explains that the book includes more genres than a writer may actually use, "the point is to find the best move for your current writing situation and try to remember successful moves for the future" (1). Here he alludes to the current research on genre and transfer, but the text is written in a simple, explanatory fashion with no citations to outside works. This is because the audience is students, and the textbook is designed to be streamlined and straightforward.

This textbook is divided into two parts. Part one is entitled "Genres" and part two is entitled "Moves." Part one presents twenty-one common genres listed in alphabetical order. These genres include abstract, annotated bibliography, application essay, application letter, argument, blog, e-mail, gripe letter, literary analysis, literature review, op-ed essay, personal essay, profile, proposal, reflection, report, response to reading, resume, review, rhetorical analysis, and wiki.

For each genre, Dethier provides a sample. He also outlines and answers questions regarding purpose, audience, content, length, arrangement, pronoun usage, tone, and potential variants. In this regard, part one serves as a useful reference guide. When a writer encounters an unfamiliar genre, this text can help her quickly identify the basic conventions of that genre. To address the wide range of the genres he includes, Dethier describes *21 Genres* as "useful to the individual writer, whether or not the writer is currently in a writing class" (5).

Some of these genres are ones that composition students are very likely to encounter when composing for a college course. Literary analysis and rhetorical analysis, for instance, are primarily academic genres. Other genres in this textbook—such as the application essay, application letter, and resume—may not fit neatly into a first-year composition curriculum. However, these genres are among the most important ones that students will write in terms of obtaining professional opportunities. And by including these genres, this textbook gains viability as a required text for not only first-year composition courses but also for professional and business writing courses. Genres such as blog and email could be written in the context of the university or could be instances of self-sponsored writing. For the email genre, Dethier urges students to analyze the writing situation, understand email as more formal than social media, and be conscious of tone. Because it identifies features of a genre that students compose every day, *21 Genres* has immediate utility.

As evidenced by the attention to blog and email genres, this textbook goes beyond print to consider genres on the web. *21 Genres* directs students to visit Wikipedia and also a technical and professional writing wiki to understand wikis as a genre. For teachers who require wiki writing, *21 Genres* is a useful starting point. Dethier provides a description of the common features of wikis and suggests moves to make in order to contribute. However, teachers will need to guide students in assessing the particular workings of specific wikis. Because different wikis have different rules, teachers may also choose to direct students to the Wikipedia page "List of wikis," which includes dozens of wikis used by various organizations for a range of purposes.

Part two contains over two hundred moves that are organized in ten chapters. The term "moves" refers to actions such as using a double-entry journal, finding a model, asking "what's not there?," using headings and subheadings, and integrating text and visuals. The introduction to part two urges writers to take on a spirit of playfulness and combine moves in new ways (151). The voice of these chapters is instructive, not judgmental, and aims to relate to students. For example, the chapter entitled "Develop" reads, "If you find yourself thinking, 'I don't have anything to say,' or 'I don't know what to say,' you should practice the moves in this chapter" (185). The chapter on "Drafting" is helpful because it explains multiple ways to draft, making visible something that is quite obvious to writing teachers—different genres necessitate different drafting strategies—but can be crucial information for student writers encountering new genres.

The information provided in the chapters of part two is highly relevant, but unfortunately these moves are a bit difficult to navigate. Moves are labeled with numbers that do not correspond to page numbers. The second part of this guide requires page flipping back to the table of contents each time the reader needs to locate an individual move. Teachers will need to spend some time showing students how to navigate the second part of this textbook.

21 Genres will function as a useful reference for college composition students. Part one serves as a clear guide for demystifying common genres that students write. However, composition instructors must keep in mind that students will need to read *many* samples of a particular genre in order to have an understanding of how that genre works (4). This book will pair well with an analysis of multiple models of a given genre. While *21 Genres* details basic conventions of each genre, it works with a highly restricted definition of genre as a form or category (3). As a result, it does not address how and when students can challenge the genres in which they so often write. Instructors may choose to balance this reference book with examples of genres that remix, parody, or redefine what constitutes genre.

Oxford, Ohio

Theorizing Histories of Rhetoric, edited by Michelle Ballif. Carbondale: SIUP, 2013. 238 pp.

Reviewed by Kevin C. Moore, University of California, Santa Barbara

Billing itself as an attempt to rewrite and retheorize Victor A. Vitanza's 1994 volume of essays *Writing Histories of Rhetoric*, Michelle Ballif's new collection *Theorizing Histories of Rhetoric* takes on an overdue sequel project in rhetorical historiography (2). To be certain, Ballif's effort to tap the *kairotic* moment of Vitanza's influential collection has an expansive set of shoes to fill. Vitanza's book emerged from a 1989 conference on the theoretical and methodological considerations underwriting the construction of rhetorical history, and it energized both the emerging field of historiography within rhetoric and composition studies and rhetorical histories themselves. The good news is that Ballif, and the impressive list of contributors she has assembled—Sharon Crowley, Jessica Enoch, Richard Leo Enos, G. L. Ercolini, Pat J. Gehrke, Debra Hawhee, Byron Hawk, Steven Mailloux, LuMing Mao, Charles E. Morris III, Christa J. Olson, K. J. Rawson, Jane S. Sutton, and Vitanza himself—successfully accomplish their primary task of reprioritizing methodological and theoretical questions through the collaborative writing of rhetorical history. Through the productive dissonance generated by the volume's diverse array of methodologies, interventions, and example histories, it also moves in directions that would have seemed impossible in the mid-nineties, presenting innovative and in some cases radically inclusive approaches. Some of the most auspicious of these were developed in response to recent debates on the archive, globalization, and queer historiographies. But *Theorizing Histories of Rhetoric* also opens wholly original questions, such as what is the appropriate scale of a rhetorical history (Hawhee; Olson), and what does it mean to think of rhetorical history with the future in mind (Ercolini; Gehrke)? Through its embrace of rhetorical history's disorder, Ballif's collection at once provides models for how to represent suppressed and marginalized archives as well as occasions for reevaluating the cultural meaning of writing histories of all kinds.

Like Vitanza's earlier book, the essays in Ballif's collection have been carefully curated to produce rich, unexpected conversations with one another (e.g., as the book's jacket material indicates, one reviewer has called the collection "a lively Symposium that recalls Plato's"). One of the most important features of *Theorizing Histories of Rhetoric* is thus the reader's experience of discovering resonance and dissonance across the various essays of the collection. Consider, for instance, how Richard Leo Enos' reminder to question textual authority in the first essay of the collection ("Theory, Validity, and the Historiography of Classical Rhetoric: A Discussion of Archaeological Rhetoric") fits into the volume at large when taken as the collection's classical figurehead. As Enos explains, fetishizing the authority of a text is a surefire way to limit one's vision when it comes to reconstructing Homeric rhetoric. While postmodern rhetoricians regularly acknowledge the limitations of the text, historians of classical rhetoric, in Enos's perception, forget that accurate representation of a particular rhetorical paradigm requires looking beyond the text to the physical and cognitive evidence of archaeological discoveries, which illustrate much about the "mentality of the time"—in this case, Ancient Greece (13–14). At first glance, Enos's proscription feels determined by the specific content of his own canonical project of rhetorical history, and hardly a general (let alone radical) principle for historiography. Enos, it seems, simply presents a method for accurately reconstructing the rhetoric of a time and place to which we have access mainly through artifacts and transcriptions of oral texts. But as one proceeds across the volume, it becomes clear that *all* of the essays in *Theorizing Histories*—even those engaging marginalized and suppressed rhetorics—provide strategies for getting beyond content analysis to questions of rhetorical situation, which are only readable when texts are considered in their larger historical contexts, and which must also take into account the position and agenda of the observer. The essays in the first half of the volume, especially, tend to follow this arc: they begin by representing their particular content—Homeric rhetoric, Jesuit rhetorical practices (Mailloux), the rhetoric of the Dao (Mao), alternative women's rhetorics (Enoch), queer archives (Morris; Rawson)—and end by proposing a general principle for how the rhetorical historian ought to approach similar archives. Significantly, these principles emerge organically from the specific projects at hand, rather than deductively or as imposed upon their content. On their own, the methodologies presented in many of the essays in Ballif's collection could seem limited to their specialized historical fields. Presented together, however, Ballif cultivates occasions for finding mutual reinforcement in unexpected places.

The most powerful chapters of the collection are those that deal most explicitly with historically marginalized, non-Western, and alternative rhetorics. LuMing Mao, for instance, shows how it is impossible to analyze the rhetoric of the *Daodejing* without learning from it, without recognizing that stable terms in the Dao are always collapsing into their opposite. To effectively represent such a rhetoric, one must cultivate an "art of recontextualization," which involves explicitly "recognizing how the conditions of the present can influence the act of representation and even perpetuate the existing power imbalances" (47). Similarly, Jessica Enoch proposes in "Releasing Hold: Feminist Historiography without the Tradition" that we approach the archive as not just an instrument to "recover women," but as a "site that creates and shapes public memories for and about women" (65); archives *structure* history as well as preserve it, and a rhetorical history must take these functions into account.

By far the most provocative historiographic method in the volume, however, appears in the chapter "Queer Archives/Archival Queers" by Charles E. Morris III and K. J. Rawson, which presents the queer archive as an especially important site for rhetorical history, as well as the possibility of becoming an "archival queer" in the writing of all rhetorical history. In Morris and Rawson's view, the massive split between the historian's view of the archive as a body of documents to be explored and the cultural theorist's view of the archive as metaphor has distracted us from considering alternative (e.g., queer) archives as "sites of rhetorical invention" (78). In our own time, when dubious heteronormative standards are no longer taken for granted, historians have an obligation to "[s]eek out affective relationships with the past" (79), with a keen eye to whether those relationships are positive or negative, a matter of "identification" or "disidentification" (80–81). How the historian relates to the past affectively, and not just objectively or rationally, is made a priority in this essay, and not only for those dealing with queer archives. Like all of the most striking essays in this collection, Morris and Rawson's take their specific approach to the archives with which they work, and present it to the reader as a universally applicable theoretical possibility.

Admittedly, and somewhat counterintuitively, the chapters of the study that might be identified as the most closely aligned with poststructuralist "high theory"—mainly the later chapters of the book—fall somewhat flat. This may be simply because they follow such a remarkable set of organic theoretical proposals, ground in the mill of their respective archives. Yet the possibility that high theory has gone a little stale is something of which the collection is aware, especially in Sharon Crowly's "Afterword," which reflects on the volume at large. Crowly explains, "Theory did not go away—this collection is rife with it . . . What is missing is the old fervor" (190). Surely it is intriguing to think of the possible implications of applying complexity theory to rhetorical history (Hawk), and a pleasure to follow the deconstructive flights of Jane S. Sutton and also Ballif herself as they explore, respectively, the figure of the "nose" of rhetoric in Aristotle (and beyond) and the possibility of "hauntological" rhetorics. This collection is at its best, however, in the essays that approach messy, incomplete, marginal archives; legitimately learn how to read them on their own terms; and thus present new, original lessons in methodology.

The greatest impact of Ballif's collection, then, may be how it challenges our notion of what constitutes "theory" in the first place. Most readers will pick up *Theorizing Histories of Rhetoric* expecting to witness new applications of canonical theorists, or new explanations of how existing theories can be useful. These moves do occur in the volume, but its most compelling moments demonstrate how marginalized and nontraditional archives can dictate new, portable methodologies for writing rhetorical history.

Santa Barbara, California

Works Cited

Vitanza, Victor. *Writing Histories of Rhetoric*. 1994. Carbondale: SIUP, 2013. Print.

Announcements

Call for Proposals – 2014 Graduate Research Network

The **Graduate Research Network (GRN)** invites proposals for its 2014 workshop, June 5, 2014, at the Computers and Writing Conference hosted by Washington State University, Pullman, WA. The C&W Graduate Research Network is an all-day pre-conference event, open to all registered conference participants at no charge. Roundtable discussions group together those with similar interests, and discussion leaders facilitate discussion and offer suggestions for developing research projects and for finding suitable venues for publication. We encourage anyone interested or involved in graduate education and scholarship—students professors, mentors, and interested others—to participate in this important event. The GRN welcomes those pursuing work at any stage, from those just beginning to consider ideas to those whose projects are ready to pursue publication. Participants are also invited to apply for travel funding through the CW/GRN Travel Grant Fund. Deadline for submissions is May 5, 2014. For more information or to submit a proposal, visit our website at http://www.gradresearchnetwork.org or email Janice Walker at jwalker@georgiasouthern.edu.

* * *

Academic Exchange Quarterly, an independent double-blind-peer-reviewed print journal, is now accepting submissions for its special section on writing center theory and practice, to be published in the winter 2014 issue (18.4). Articles may explore issues of theory, practice, and experience in writing center work, including qualitative and empirical studies and discussions of pedagogy.

Articles may also consider the following: How writing center professionals cope with change and the eventuality of needing to expand their efforts in response to new economic and demographic challenges. Furthermore, as we move towards increasingly virtual and technologically dependent learning communities, how can these efforts help meet the evolving demands of our students?

In addition to writing center directors and other administrators, we welcome submissions from professional staff, faculty tutors, and graduate students who work in a writing center (see special instructions for graduate students: http://rapidintellect.com/AEQweb/rufengs.htm). Manuscript length should be between 2,000 and 3,000 words. Please identify your submission with the keyword "Center-2."

Every published article automatically qualifies for inclusion in the forth-coming book, *Writing Center Theory and Practice*, edited by Kellie A. Charron and published by the Sound Instruction series.

Submissions will be accepted until the end of August; however, early submissions are encouraged as they offer the following incentives:

- longer time for revision
- opportunity to be considered for Editor's Choice
- eligibility to have article's abstract and/or full text posted on journal's main webpage
- opportunity to be considered for inclusion in Sound Instruction Series

For more information, please visit http://www.rapidintellect.com/AEQweb/center2.htm, or email Feature Editor and Sound Instruction Book Editor Kellie Charron at kajr10@comcast.net.

Contributors

Tabetha Adkins is Assistant Professor of English and WPA at Texas A&M University-Commerce. She received her PhD from the University of Louisville in 2009 and studies literacy and writing.

Marsha Lee Baker, an Associate Professor at Western Carolina University, teaches rhetoric, writing, and critical studies. Her scholarship involves nonviolent rhetorics and peaceable pedagogies, including articles in collections published by Boynton/Cook and NCTE, in *Virginia English Bulletin* and *English Journal*, and at CCCC, NCTE, and Feminisms and Rhetorics.

Cheryl E. Ball is associate professor of digital publishing at West Virginia University. Since 2006, Ball has been editor of *Kairos: Rhetoric, Technology, and Pedagogy*. Her research on multimodal composition, digital media publishing and editing, and university writing pedagogy can be found, mostly for free, on her website: http://ceball.com.

Kristine L. Blair is Professor and Chair of the Department of English at Bowling Green State University, where she teaches digital rhetoric and scholarly publication courses in the Rhetoric and Writing Doctoral Program. She currently serves as editor of both *Computers and Composition* print and *Computers and Composition Online*.

David Blakesley is the Robert S. Campbell Chair in Technical Communication and Professor of English at Clemson University, where he also serves as the Faculty Representative to the Board of Trustees. He is the publisher and founder of Parlor Press (http://www.parlorpress.com), now in its twelfth year. He is also the editor of *KB Journal* and (with Dawn Formo and Jeremy Tirrell) *The Writing Instructor*.

Kevin Brock is an Assistant Professor of English at the University of South Carolina. He primarily studies the rhetorical qualities and possibilities of software code as compositional practice and text.

Eric Dieter is Director of Pre-College Academic Readiness Programs in the Division of Diversity and Community Engagement at UT-Austin. In addition to implementing college-level credit opportunities at high schools whose students are underrepresented in postsecondary education, his research interests include expanding the civic, scholastic, and pedagogic understanding and usefulness of ethos.

Gretchen L. Dietz is a doctoral student in composition and rhetoric at Miami University in Oxford, Ohio. She teaches courses in first-year and advanced composition. Her research focuses on composition studies and style.

Zachary Dobbins is an Assistant Professor of Rhetoric at Eckerd College. He is the 2004-2005 recipient of the Maxine Hairston Prize for Excellence in Teaching from the Department of Rhetoric and Writing at UT-Austin, where he received his PhD. His research interests include empathy, critical thinking, and the novelist Russell Banks.

Douglas Eyman teaches courses in digital rhetoric, technical editing, and professional writing at George Mason University. Eyman is the senior editor and publisher of *Kairos: A Journal of Rhetoric, Technology, and Pedagogy*, an online journal that has been publishing peer-reviewed scholarship on computers and writing in born-digital formats since 1996.

Adam Frelin received a BFA from Indiana University of Pennsylvania, and an MFA from the University of California, San Diego. He has shown his work widely at venues such as the Los Angeles County Museum of Art, Getty Research Institute, Aldrich Contemporary Art Museum, and Contemporary Art Museum St. Louis.

Gail Hawisher is University Distinguished Scholar and Professor Emeritus of English at the University of Illinois, Urbana-Champaign. Her work probes the many connections between literate activity and digital media as reflected most recently in her coauthored *Transnational Literate Lives in Digital Times*, a multimodal, born-digital study of literacy practices across the world.

Justin Hodgson is an Assistant Professor of English at Indiana University and founding editor of *The Journal for Undergraduate Multimedia Projects* (*TheJUMP*). He has published digital and print works on multimedia scholarship, professional rhetorics, gaming pedagogy, and rhetoric, technology, and culture.

Jo Mackiewicz moved to the Rhetoric and Professional Communication program at Iowa State University in May 2014. Her research focuses on politeness and credibility in evaluative texts such as editor-writer sessions, writing tutor-student conferences, and online reviews of technical products. She is the series editor of the ATTW Book Series in Technical and Professional Communication.

Connie Meyer received her PhD from Texas Christian University in 2012 and studies Medieval Renaissance Literature and Science Writing.

Kevin C. Moore is a Lecturer in the writing program at the University of California, Santa Barbara. His research interests include writing studies, American literature, and American intellectual history. His current book project reexamines writer's block as an American cultural myth. His work has appeared in journals including *Arizona Quarterly* and *MAKE*.

Shakil Rabbi is a PhD student in rhetoric and composition in the Department of English, Pennsylvania State University. From Bangladesh, he is interested in the rhetoric of globalization, multilingual writing, higher education, and the intersection between rhetorical and postcolonial theory. He teaches undergraduate general composition courses and writing in the social sciences.

Cynthia Selfe is Co-founder and Executive Editor of Computers and Composition Digital Press/Utah State University Press with Gail Hawisher, and the Co-Founder and Co-Director of the Digital Archive of Literacy Narratives with H. Lewis Ulman. Selfe's work focuses on intersections of humans, computers, communication, teaching, and learning.

Isabelle Thompson is now retired, but until 2009, she was the coordinator of the English Center, for many years the only writing center on the Auburn University campus. Since 2005, her research has been in writing center theory and practice, especially applications related to educational theory and assessment.

Matthew Vetter is a doctoral candidate in English at Ohio University, where he teaches writing and serves as Assistant Director of Composition. His research interests include writing in online spaces, new media, composition theory and pedagogy, and curriculum development. He's also something of a Wikipedia fanatic.

Christian Weisser is an Associate Professor of English at Penn State Berks, where he coordinates the Professional Writing Program and the Writing Across the Curriculum Program. Christian is the editor of *Composition Forum*, and his current research focuses on the intersections between ecology, sustainability, and writing.

Carl Whithaus studies the impact of information technologies on literacy practices, writing in the disciplines and professions, and writing assessment. His books include *Writing Across Distances and Disciplines* (Erlbaum/Routledge, 2008), *Teaching and Evaluating Writing in the Age of Computers and High-Stakes Testing* (Erlbaum, 2005), and *Multimodal Literacies and Emerging Genres* (Pittsburgh, 2013).

BGSU®

Rhetoric & Writing PhD Program

Preparing Rhetoric and Composition Faculty for over 30 Years

Since its founding in 1980, Bowling Green State University's program has prepared about ninety graduates for faculty careers in rhetoric and composition. Students and faculty in the Rhetoric & Writing PhD Program are committed scholar-teachers who utilize a range of approaches—rhetorical, cultural, empirical, technological—that characterize rhetoric and composition in the twenty-first century.

Some highlights of the Rhetoric & Writing PhD Program:
- Eight core courses in history, theory, digital rhetorics, research methods, scholarly publication, and composition studies as a discipline, plus electives in rhetoric and composition and related areas of scholarly interest to students.
- Professional development involving mentoring, collaboration, a monthly colloquium series, and post-prelim groups emphasizing dissertation progress and the job search.
- Varied assistantship assignments (FYW, intermediate writing, writing center, faculty research, editorial work, program administration, community outreach, etc.) and competitive non-service fellowships in the fourth year of funding.
- Four-year graduation rate typical for full-time students.
- Placement rate among program graduates approaching 100%.

Rhetoric & Writing PhD Program
http://www.bgsu.edu/departments/english/rcweb/index.html
Facebook Group: BGSU Rhetoric & Writing

Program Director, Sue Carter Wood
carters@bgsu.edu
English Graduate Office: 419-372-6864